Further praise for **The Business of Influence**

"*The Business of Influence* is a whack on the side of the head for traditional marketers. By focusing on influence, instead of traditional marketing think, it reframes and redefines everything that a modern marketer does. *The Business of Influence* should be found, dog-eared and jam-packed with marks in the margins on every successful CMO's desk."
Katie Delahaye Paine, Founder and CEO, KD Paine & Partners, author *Measure What Matters*

"Philip Sheldrake shares an important vision of the new communications world order. PR and advertising professionals need to sit up and take note. Influence is the future watchword – and the smart companies are already exploring it and switching models."
Robert Phillips, President & CEO EMEA, Edelman

"Today, every organization is in the influence business. We influence customers to buy from us, employees to work for us, and the media to write about us. Gone are the days when you could be your own island. Now, to be successful, you need to live within the influence ecosystem and that requires a change of mindset. Fortunately, Philip Sheldrake will show you how."
David Meerman Scott, bestselling author of *The New Rules of Marketing & PR* **and the new hit** *Real-Time Marketing & PR*

"Philip Sheldrake helps us rethink the business of influence. It goes without saying that the social web has transformed the world. Business strategies need to keep pace. Readers should embrace this book and let it challenge their beliefs about the future of marketing and business."
David Alston, CMO, Radian6

"Philip Sheldrake was a feisty, thoughtful and passionate audience participant during the AMEC session defining the Barcelona Principles in 2010. His belief that communications needs to change continues in this book, which gives conventional thinking a healthy stir. This is a book I hope major corporations will put on the recommended reading list for their senior management."
Barry Leggetter, Executive Director, the International Association for Measurement and Evaluation of Communication (AMEC)

"*The Business of Influence* is an excellent guide to understanding how to develop and drive a management agenda through marketing and communications in the increasingly complex age of social media and digital technology. It is a handy and useful guidebook for every practitioner from the newly minted account leader in an agency to the seasoned professional or academic in this field."
David B. Rockland, PhD; Partner, Ketchum Communications; CEO, Ketchum Pleon Change and Ketchum Global Research; Chair, AMEC US Agency Research Leaders Group

"Philip has touched a nerve with *The Business of Influence*. It's a highly detailed, authoritative examination on the business of influence, a book of the now. Many unkind observers of the current state of PR suggest it has entered a new age of snake oil sales folk. Sheldrake's book proves that there is a higher level of thought. It structures a practical study of material which I am sure will prove to be invaluable insight."
Mark Borkowski, Founder and MD, Borkowski

"*The Business of Influence* is an essential read for communications professionals seeking to keep pace with the new realities of social business. Philip Sheldrake powerfully deconstructs old business paradigms about business marketing and communications in order to align it with the realities of social business so we, as an industry, can rebuild with greater success. It can help the influence professional directly impact the bottom line in this new social media driven world."
Vanessa DiMauro, CEO Leader Networks

"Philip Sheldrake stalks the world of PR in which digital mediation is taken as a given. The nature of a web of communication is complicated and with Philip's help, we are beginning to understand how information flows through it."
David Phillips, FIPR, FSNCR, co-author of *Online Public Relations: A Practical Guide to Developing an Online Strategy in the World of Social Media*

"Philip Sheldrake gets it. Public Relations and Marketing have always been about influence and his Six Influence Flows and the Influence Scorecard are a real step forward in making sense and evaluating these activities in the digital age."
Professor Anne Gregory PhD, Director, Centre for Public Relations Studies, Leeds Business School; author *Public Relations in Practice*

"Yesterday's approaches to influence do not work in today's world. In *The Business of Influence*, Philip Sheldrake nails the fundamental problem in the 21st Century – our methods are rooted in the 20th Century."
Marshall Sponder, The Web Analytics Guru, author *Social Media Analytics*

THE BUSINESS OF INFLUENCE

To my wife Jay – the primary influence
in sparking my interest in the business of influence.

THE BUSINESS
OF INFLUENCE

REFRAMING MARKETING AND PR

FOR THE DIGITAL AGE

PHILIP SHELDRAKE

A John Wiley & Sons, Ltd., Publication

Library of Congress Cataloging-in-Publication Data

Sheldrake, Philip, 1971-
  The business of influence : reframing marketing and PR for the Digital Age /
Philip Sheldrake.
    p. cm.
  Includes bibliographical references and index.
  ISBN 978-0-470-97862-7
 1. Internet marketing. 2. Marketing. 3. Public relations.
4. Influence (Psychology) I. Title.
  HF5415.1265.S53 2011
  658.8'72—dc22

                                                          2011007714

A catalogue record for this book is available from the British Library.

ISBN 978-0-470-97862-7 (hardback) ISBN 978-1-119-97337-9 (ebk)
ISBN 978-1-119-97830-5 (ebk) ISBN 978-1-119-97831-2 (ebk)

Set in 10 on 14.5 pt FF Scala by Toppan Best-set Premedia Limited, Hong Kong
Printed in Great Britain by TJ International Ltd, Padstow, Cornwall, UK

CONTENTS

FOREWORD

This book will make practitioners in marketing, PR, advertising, communications, and any professional with the word digital in his title uncertain about the future of his discipline. Philip Sheldrake makes the case that the traditional boundaries of these professions must morph into a more holistic expertise, which he calls the influence professional. And while such professionals must retain their creative right-brain talents, they must become far more skilled in left-brained analytical competencies.

The convergence of markets, media, and technology raises the bar further. New business models, the proliferation of social media, the relative power shift from producers to consumers, and the overwhelming amount of structured and unstructured data make managing our businesses more challenging than ever. It seems that we increasingly know more and more about less and less. Change is constant, and accelerating.

What to do? The author proposes a creative, structured approach to the business of influence, which is to say, business itself. He identifies the interactions between stakeholders – businesses, employees, customers, competitors – and maps the primary influence flows among them. He provides a practical framework for seeing, and acting on, the drivers of value creation. He proposes an Influence Scorecard that integrates strategy, objectives, and processes in an actionable influence framework. The scorecard provides structure, focus, and a common language – across organizational boundaries – that drives desired behaviors and outcomes. It puts influence at the center of the strategy.

Strategy is how an organization intends to create value for its stakeholders consistent with its mission. Strategy is a process, and like any process, it must be managed and its efficacy measured. And while strategy is important, it's the execution that counts. In a world where 7 out of 10 organizations fail to execute their strategies, it is not surprising that execution – that is, fulfilling the promise of creating value for stakeholders – is the number one issue that keeps executives up at night. The Kaplan Norton Balanced Scorecard has become the dominant framework successful organizations use to execute their strategies.

The author's Influence Scorecard builds on the Kaplan Norton approach, in which success is based on universal management principles: aligning around the critical few things that matter, identifying cause-and-effect relationships that result in desired outcomes, setting measures and targets to drive behaviors, choosing initiatives that close performance gaps, and managing strategy as a process. The Influence Scorecard shares these principles with the Balanced Scorecard, and applies them to the emergent, cross-disciplinary domain of influence.

Readers will find helpful the author's syntheses of recent research and writing in the art and science of influence – including insights into social media and Web 3.0 developments, chapter summaries, and a glossary. Whether the emerging profession of the Chief Influence Officer leads the nexus of influence as the author suggests, or another C level executive, influence – like strategy itself – is a team sport. Influence is everyone's responsibility. This book will help you understand your contribution to that reality.

Robert L. Howie, Jr.
Managing Director, CMO, Palladium Group, Inc.
Director, Kaplan Norton Balanced Scorecard Hall of Fame
for Executing Strategy
Boston, Massachusetts
February 2011

ACKNOWLEDGEMENTS

Jay O'Connor, Robert Howie, Doc Searls, Katie Delahaye Paine, David Meerman Scott, Barry Leggetter, Jay Krall, Stephen Waddington, Robert Phillips, Gabbi Cahane, David Phillips, Giles Palmer, Andrew Bruce Smith, Julio Romo, Ted Shelton, Blaise Hammond, Steve Earl, Scott Monty, Brian Solis, John Woodget, Andrew Betts, Claire Plimmer, Richard Wood.

INTRODUCTION

A re you in the business of influence?
You have been influenced when you think in a way you wouldn't otherwise have thought, or when you do something you wouldn't otherwise have done.

So, are you influencing? And are you being influenced?

If you're in the business of marketing, advertising, public relations, internal communications, public affairs, customer service, customer relationship management, social media, copywriting and content, SEO, branding, branded apps and widgets, brand journalism, Web design, graphic design, direct marketing, packaging, merchandising, promotion, publicity, events, sponsorship, sales and sales promotion, marketing and market research, product and service design and development, then you're in the business of influence.

In fact, if you're in business, indeed any type of organization, then you're in the business of influence.

This book contends that the business of influence is broken. At least that's how the popular press might report it. If you want to consider it through the lens of more cerebral media, you'd say that the current strategic approach to influence and the structure, processes and evaluation of influence are not fit for purpose. If the business of influence were to suddenly occur to us right now, relieving us for one hypothetical moment of the historic baggage of past political, economic, social and technological forces, traditions, language and happenstance, we'd suggest something quite different. It would take much greater advantage of the capabilities of the latest information technology and be far better aligned to its *raison d'être* courtesy of recent insights into business strategy.

We need such a rethink. Not for academic purposes. Not for 'wouldn't it be nice if' daydreaming. But for real, practical application to improve operational effectiveness and efficiency and to delight more stakeholders more often and more profitably.

We need such a rethink because information technology has revolutionized communications, massively and irrevocably. The authors of the *Cluetrain Manifesto* asserted back in 1999 that the Internet allows markets to revert to the days when a market was defined by people gathering and talking among themselves about buyer and seller reputation, product quality and prices. This was lost for a while as the scale of organizations and markets outstripped the facility for consumers to coalesce. But the consumers' conversation and participation are now well and truly re-ignited, and the mechanics, the variables and parameters of the ebb and flow of influence within each and every market have been transformed.

Moreover, we're only a fraction of the way through this information technology revolution. Things are about to get faster.

This book explains where we've come from and where we're heading. It identifies the changes that organizations and individual practitioners must pursue to remain relevant and delight those stakeholders more often and more profitably, and provides a roadmap from here to there.

This book is about your organization, your profession and your career. As with all changes to the competitive landscape, the earliest adopters and adapters will secure competitive advantage for their organization and for themselves, while the laggards will suffer competitive disadvantage. And quickly.

The questions this book seeks to answer

In rethinking the modern processes of influence, we address four big questions:

1. Following the rise of social media, how can we make sense of the noise in our marketplace to help us to achieve our objectives and beat our competitors?

2. How should the influence processes permeate the organization more systematically and measurably, accruing its practitioners more authority and accountability in the boardroom?
3. What big trends must everyone in the business of influence get to grips with?
4. Who does this stuff? What traits and skills are demanded of the modern practitioner?

Let's take a very brief look at each question:

Q1. Following the rise of social media, how can we make sense of the noise in our marketplace to help us to achieve our objectives and beat our competitors?

Social media has ascended so quickly that today only a minority media remain without a social component. The Six Influence Flows™ provides a new model for the ways in which the motivating and deterring influence factors go around and come around, addressing every stakeholder – a model that can then inform your organization's structural and cultural design.

We review the current state of integrated marketing communications and the latest and imminent innovations in social Web analytics. We introduce the ethics of analytics, and make the argument that you should invest as much resource into being influenced as you dedicate to influencing others – after all, improving your sensitivity to your stakeholders' thoughts and feelings can only improve your abilities to address their needs and concerns, and live up to their desires and aspirations more diligently. It stands to reason.

Q2. How should the influence processes permeate the organization more systematically and measurably, accruing its practitioners more authority and accountability in the boardroom?

I introduce the Influence Scorecard™. Named in homage to the Balanced Scorecard approach to business performance management, it's a management approach rather than a yardstick per se. It helps an organization to identify which influence processes it wishes to differentiate to its competitive advantage (its influence strategy) and helps to translate influence (marketing, PR, customer service, etc.) objectives into operational objectives, plans and action, potentially demanding new or revised structures and processes.

We discuss what constitutes best practice in measurement and evaluation, and the nature of complexity and chaos in your marketplace. We differentiate between influencer-centric and influence-centric measurement. We show how the Influence Scorecard guides the selection of measurement criteria and the ways in which these measurements can be made and presented for incorporation into business performance management (BPM) approaches such as the Balanced Scorecard.

The Influence Scorecard informs the mechanism for learning from these measures and adjusting influence tactics and strategy accordingly. Importantly, it finally puts to rest the seemingly unending debate about return on investment in the context of marketing and PR type activities.

Q3. What big trends must everyone in the business of influence get to grips with?

We're in fast-moving times, but the candidates for 'big trends' stand out clearly. First, there's the mobile phone, and smartphones more specifically. And this takes us quickly on to all the other things we're all interacting with today and tomorrow – the so-called Internet of Things.

This segues neatly into the fresh imperatives of privacy and data ownership, before we take a leap a little further into the future with the advent of buyer marketing. We complete the big trends with an introduction to the semantic Web (a.k.a. Web 3.0).

Q4. Who does this stuff? What traits and skills are demanded of the modern practitioner?

I introduce the Chief Influence Officer and the influence professional.

The influence professional represents the convergence of the historically siloed disciplines that exert influence on stakeholders and need to be influenced by stakeholders – PR, marketing, customer service, HR, operations, etc.

Influence professionals understand every option at their disposal to influence and be influenced, and are trained in selecting the right mix of the right approaches at the right time, marking possibly the most distinct departure from the traditional marketing processes manifest to date.

Incumbents know the state of all Six Influence Flows with all key stakeholders at any point in time, and evangelize and embed the Influence Scorecard approach. They are sensitized to their organizations' environments and their organizations' responses to them in a way that makes many CMOs, for example, look as if they work in little bubbles today.

The business context

The marketing and PR professions remain relatively unscientific. They are almost the last business disciplines to be transformed by information and communication technologies, and are now going through the same technology-fuelled convulsions that accounting, manufacturing, logistics and retail, for example, underwent in previous decades.

The structure, processes and too frequently blinkered specialism of its practitioners hold back most marketing and PR teams from recognizing that their objectives, activity and associated measurement and evaluation, must work in orchestrated harmony with other disciplines to deliver specific business outcomes. It is still too common, for example, to hear a practitioner or senior manager say that PR and customer service are two separate functions, or fail to gel marketing and PR with product development. If that's not frustrating enough, even getting marketing and PR to work together beautifully can be difficult.

This disorder is increasingly recognized as such, particularly as newer digital aspects bring new types of personality into marketing and PR roles (which is how I, a Chartered Engineer, came to be in this position). The more adaptable practitioners and informed management are beginning to look for new ways to define and synchronize these essential functions and interweave them more closely into the human and informational fabric of an organization.

And not a moment too soon.

The information and communication technology industry's relentless progression is accelerating. All kinds of organizations continue to embrace technology to create new revenue opportunities, improve productivity and communicate with stakeholders. Consumers continue their aggressive adoption of information and communication technology powered products and services, with the inevitable continued evolution of their individual and collective behaviours.

Web 2.0 rocked marketing and PR, but so-called Web 3.0 is already in the ascendancy. If Web 2.0 is about social participation and (user generated) content, Web 3.0 – more precisely known as the semantic Web – entails the Web understanding the meaning of this participation and content. Wikipedia is undergoing a semantic Web transformation right now, an initiative known as dbpedia. The BBC and the UK Government are already there with the bbc.co.uk and data.gov.uk websites respectively, as is Tesco with some of its websites. Tests show that Google has already tweaked its PageRank algorithm (which determines the search results returned in response to a search query) to boost the rankings of semantically marked-up content over equivalent non-semantic content,[1] constituting one serious reason by itself for marketers to understand what's going on here.

What about the Internet of Things, the term describing the connection of devices to the Internet beyond the typical computer and smartphone? In 2008 Fiat introduced the facility for drivers of some of its vehicles to collect data about their driving style, upload it to the Web and share that information with the company. Nike and Apple joined forces that same year to facilitate the collection, analysis and social sharing of personal performance data in running and other sports. Samsung and others now make Internet TVs capable of collecting data about viewing habits that can be directed into a recommendation engine. Walmart widened the focus of its RFID[2] (digital tags often attached to pallets, boxes and products) rollout from its distribution centres to its stores back in 2007, and Tesco has employed RFID since 2003.

This technological, commercial and cultural revolution is playing out today, yet many organizations still use the structure they have used for many years for their sales, operations, customer service, marketing and PR teams, and external agency, the same marketing strategies (except for the addition of Facebook and Twitter 'strategies'), and the same marketing processes and soft integration with the wider organizations.

The most dynamic and successful organizations are beginning to explore different ways of working, making the status quo simply untenable for all organizations and marketing professionals in the medium term.

Influenceprofessional.com

Better a book go unread than fail to influence the reader – then the author has wasted the reader's time too.

We have been influenced when we think in a way we wouldn't otherwise have thought, or when we do something we wouldn't otherwise have done. In seeking then to nourish that thinking and focus that action, this book is accompanied by a website at www.influenceprofessional.com. It aspires to be a community-driven website that aims to:

- provide a discussion forum pivoting around the opinions and assertions presented in this book and associated perspectives and thought leadership from other sources;
- cultivate agreement on what skills the influence professional must have, and what might be nice-to-haves, with links to books, blogs, training collateral, events and other resources;
- give aspiring influence professionals the opportunity to ask questions of experts and each other, and share their experiences.

I do hope you have the time and energy to join in. I very much look forward to meeting you, learning what you think about this book and learning from your experiences and insights.

1

When I first mooted this book with friends and associates in the marketing and PR profession, a common thread emerged in response. Although it was expressed in many different ways, it boiled down to this: there's change fatigue.

The marketing and PR professional has had to get to grips with quite a lot during the past decade, and this section aims to provide a whistle-stop tour of that journey and where we find ourselves today, but in that response lies the answer.

Change in business should never be for the sake of change. Change has been demanded of marketing, public relations, customer service and other aspects of business by social, technological, environmental, legal and economic factors, and the marketing, PR and other professionals have reacted with varying degrees of success – reactive change.

This book, however, is championing proactive change – proactive in consolidating the multiple adaptations made reactively, and proactive in restructuring, repositioning, regearing and empowering the influence processes as organizational lifeblood, delivering competitive advantage for the organization and the individual practitioner.

Of course, laggards to this opportunity will find themselves having to react. Such is life.

Let's look a bit more closely at where marketing and PR are today.

The Cluetrain and Permission Marketing

The *Cluetrain Manifesto*[3] and *Permission Marketing*,[4] both of 1999, were the first signposts that the status quo of marketing and public relations was about to end, and relatively abruptly. And from a personal perspective that was just fine – I was still in my twenties with comparatively little marketing and PR experience, so I was joining advantageously at just the moment when the rules were changing.

With a collection of assertions and a call to action, the *Cluetrain* authors painted a frank, unambiguous vision of the way in which the Internet would affect the way in which individuals communicate and organize, and the responses this revolution would demand of organizations.

> A powerful global conversation has begun. Through the Internet, people are discovering and inventing new ways to share relevant knowledge with blinding speed. As a direct result, markets are getting smarter – and getting smarter faster than most companies.
>
> These markets are conversations. Their members communicate in language that is natural, open, honest, direct, funny and often shocking. Whether explaining or complaining, joking or serious, the human voice is unmistakably genuine. It can't be faked.

The authors, Rick Levine, Christopher Locke, Doc Searls and David Weinberger, created a storm. On one side, the so-called digerati fanned the flames and, some would say, adopted the *Manifesto* quasi-religiously. The sceptics on the other side called the whole thing a cult and claimed that not much would change in the long run. The detractors contended that it was more hype than substance, much like the 'dotcom' bubble that was inflating and then popping around them at the time.

The detractors were wrong.

Consumers today check how others rate products and services before taking the plunge themselves, and they share their thoughts for outstanding and substandard service openly and with brutal honesty. The term 'conversational marketing' is now considered by many marketing and PR firms to be a core service or skill, and there is hardly a marketing or PR expert who doesn't chime up with the need for brands to be authentic or open or transparent – words that were applied considerably less often in this context during the 20th century. Information and communication technologies, and the corresponding cultural shifts, have, as the *Cluetrain* authors put it, rekindled 'human to human' conversations. 'Markets are conversations.' The inference is simply that this marks the end of the 'us and them' divide, or big corporate 'versus' the little guy.

As a compliment to the *Cluetrain* authors' focus on dialogue and public relations, Seth Godin's *Permission Marketing* attacked the sacred cow, advertising:

> You can define advertising as the science of creating and placing media that interrupts the consumer and then gets him or her to take some action. That's quite a lot to ask of thirty seconds of TV time or twenty-five square inches of the newspaper, but without interruption there's no chance of action, and without action advertising flops. . . .
>
> The ironic thing is that marketers have responded to this problem with the single worst cure possible. To deal with the clutter and the diminished effectiveness of Interruption Marketing, they're interrupting us even more!

And according to Kantar Media (formerly TNS Media Intelligence), advertising spend in the USA has grown further since then, albeit with some ups and downs mirroring the booms and busts along the way, from an inflation adjusted[5] $115.1 billion in 1999[6] when *Permission Marketing* hit the bookshops, to $125.3 billion in 2009.[7] Kantar Media reports 14 minutes of network ad messages per hour of prime time US network TV in Q4 2009, with a further 5 and 15 minutes of 'brand appearances' for scripted and unscripted programming, respectively. So, even more interruption?

Yet Eric Clemons, Professor of Operations and Information Management at The Wharton School of the University of Pennsylvania, penned a polemic for TechCrunch in March 2009 in which he asserts that advertising will fail because consumers do not trust it, they don't want to view it, and mostly they don't need it.[8]

Godin champions a new marketing approach substituting permission for interruption, and interestingly his four tests of permission marketing ended up bearing more than a passing resemblance to facets of public relations:

1. *Does every single marketing effort you create encourage a learning relationship with your customers? Does it invite customers to 'raise their hands' and start communicating?*

2. *Do you have a permission database? Do you track the number of people who have given you permission to communicate with them?*

3. *If consumers gave you permission to talk to them, would you have anything to say? Have you developed a marketing curriculum to teach people about your products?*

4. *Once people become customers, do you work to deepen your permission to communicate with those people?*

Hugh MacLeod pulls no punches, as cartoonists are want to do: 'If you talked to people the way advertising talked to people, they'd punch you in the face.'[9]

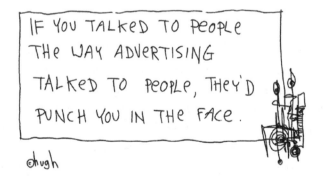

By 2006, those sceptics of the social Web revolution were increasingly subdued or simply converted. *Time Magazine* chose 'You' as Time Person of the Year, representing the millions of social media participants. Facebook removed its prior membership restrictions, opening its service up to everyone, and YouTube was the fastest growing Web service ever. The *Wall Street Journal* reported that YouTube was consuming more Internet capacity by its second birthday in 2007 than the entire Internet had in 2000[10] . . . even the British Royal Family got itself a YouTube channel[11] in 2007.

At the Association of National Advertisers annual conference that year, A.G. Lafley, the Chief Executive of Procter & Gamble, said: 'Consumers are beginning in a very real sense to own our brands and participate in their creation . . . We need to learn to begin to let go.'[12] David Meerman Scott then described the fall of traditional mass media marketing, and crystallized the ramifications, opportunities and challenges for the marketing and PR world with *The New Rules of Marketing and PR*.[13] It became an international best seller, available in some 26 languages.

A decade may feel like a long time when you're in it, but historically one can only conclude that we have just witnessed an unprecedented, massive, fast and irreversible transformation.

Perhaps you might interpret the 9% hike in US ad spend in the decade to 2009 as proof that nothing has changed; or perhaps that advertising is migrating away from spray 'n' pray to a more intelligent, targeted and responsive model; or perhaps that marketers are panicking; or perhaps that new digital ad formats have just been too tempting, or indeed an improvement on the old straightforward interruption. Fortunately, we don't need to answer that question here. We simply have to view the matter through the eyes and ears of your customers and other stakeholders, who make no informed distinction between different marketing and communications methods, only knowing what they like, listening when you respond to their questions and points of view and needs and aspirations, and filtering out the rest.

Marketing and public relations

Most readers of this book will be working in, studying, teaching or researching marketing and/or PR. Others will be working in other disciplines central to influence, such as sales and customer service, or senior management figures or management consultants keeping up with the latest ideas. Regardless, I hope you won't mind if we invest some time defining both marketing and PR. Why? Well, this book wants to map out a journey from A to B, and navigating to B is so much easier if we're all at A to begin with. Moreover, experts don't agree . . .

Marketing

In its 2009 paper, *Marketing and the 7Ps*,[14] the Chartered Institute of Marketing (CIM) defines marketing as 'the management process responsible for identifying, anticipating and satisfying customer requirements profitably'. The paper continues:

> ... the customer is at the heart of marketing, and businesses ignore this at their peril.
>
> In essence, the marketing function is the study of market forces and factors and the development of a company's position to optimise its benefit from them. It is all about getting the right product or service to the customer at the right price, in the right place, at the right time. Both business history and current practice remind us that without proper marketing, companies cannot get close to customers and satisfy their needs. And if they don't, a competitor surely will.

However, the CIM recognized in its 2007 *Tomorrow's World*[15] paper that its definition harks back to 1976 and could do with an update. The paper identifies a number of reasons why a revision may be needed, including:

- The discipline has become more sophisticated, possibly demanding subdivision into three broad paths: science, arts and humanities
- The idea that marketing is no longer a separate role but something everyone in an organization does to a greater or lesser degree
- The technology revolution has altered the dynamic between an organization and its customers, increasing the power of the customer (the rebalancing we referred to earlier in this chapter)
- The fragmentation of media and the increasing resistance of audiences to marketing communications
- The increasing need for numeracy and research fluency
- The role of people management in the marketing skill set.

While the following definition was mooted in the paper, the CIM does not yet appear to have officially adopted it, or one based on it:

The strategic business function that creates value by stimulating, facilitating and fulfilling customer demand.

It does this by building brands, nurturing innovation, developing relationships, creating good customer service and communicating benefits.

With a customer-centric view, marketing brings positive return on investment, satisfies shareholders and stakeholders from business and the community, and contributes to positive behavioural change and a sustainable business future.

The definition given in what many consider the seminal marketing textbook, *Principles of Marketing*,[16] is:

Broadly defined, marketing is a social and managerial process by which individuals and groups obtain what they need and want through creating and exchanging products and value with others. In a narrower business context, marketing involves building profitable, value-laden exchange relationships with customers. Hence, we define marketing as the process by which companies create value for customers and build strong customer relationships in order to capture value from customers in return.

The American Marketing Association did, however, find itself a new definition in 2007, but to fairly widespread derision:

Marketing is the activity, set of institutions and processes for creating, communicating, delivering and exchanging offerings that have value for customers, clients, partners and society at large.

From my reading various reactions I can say that Mike Smock's blog post, 'Everything that is wrong with marketing can be found in AMA's new definition,'[17] appears to best capture the mood of those critical of the new definition. The primary criticism appears to be that, unlike CIM's current and drafted definitions – or indeed that provided in *Principles of Marketing* – the AMA fails to be explicit about marketing's role in contributing to the achievement of a for-profit organization's financial objectives.

The bit about 'society at large' also appears to have ruffled feathers as being too distanced from the cut and thrust of business, but from my perspective it's just one sign of many that marketing fancies itself as the guardian of all things in public relations. The CIM draft definition includes 'developing relationships'. The CIM paper, *Marketing and the 7Ps*, lists PR under the fourth marketing 'P', promotion.[18] And its paper, *Tomorrow's World*, clearly references PR to mean spin (spin a yarn, make up a story) rather than anything public relations experts would recognize.[19]

Public relations

I discuss PR with many people in my professional life and find that the majority only have a tenuous grasp of what PR actually encompasses, and many others simply have no idea or, worse, have it wrong. And, as we've seen, that includes professional marketers.

Believe it or not, I've met people who think PR stands for press release. And perhaps I should get over myself, but I have never liked the turn of phrase 'to PR' something. But by far the most common mistake I find is considering PR to be synonymous with media relations – journalist lunches and column inches.

I often start by telling people what PR is not. PR is not marketing. PR is not promotion (coupons, offers, etc.). For more on 'what PR is not', I found a similar list by Bill Sledzik on his blog *ToughSledding*.[20]

The PR role encompasses aspects of publicity and many people referred to as PR practitioners invest much of their time wielding the tools of publicity: (press releases, pitches, interviews,) etc. (indeed, this aspect has been referred to as 'marketing public relations', which either confuses the matter or clarifies it, depending on your point of view[21]). James Grunig's and Todd Hunt's '4 Models', first presented in 1984,[22] describe four views of public relations, the first of which is publicity or 'press agentry'. The second is known as the public information model, the third asymmetric persuasion, and the fourth the two-way symmetrical model.

The renowned *Excellence* study emphasized the fourth model and defined PR as[23]:

> a management function that focuses on two-way communication and fostering of mutually beneficial relationships between an organization and its publics.

The Public Relations Society of America puts it simply[24]:

> Public relations helps an organization and its publics adapt mutually to each other.

Terry Flynn, Fran Gregory and Jean Valin actually set up a wiki[25] to record various definitions and collaborate on consolidating a new definition for adoption at the Canadian Public Relations Society national board meeting February 2009[26]:

> Public relations is the strategic management of relationships between an organization and its diverse publics, through the use of communications, to achieve mutual understanding, realize organizational goals, and serve the public interest.

And according to the UK's Chartered Institute of Public Relations (CIPR):

> PR is the discipline that looks after reputation, with the aim of earning understanding and support and influencing opinion and behaviour. It is the planned and sustained effort to establish and maintain goodwill and mutual understanding between an organization and its publics.

In a conversation with me, Jay O'Connor, CIPR President 2010, extended this definition by stressing the role that public relations must play at board level, helping to explore, define, plan and execute strategy. She particularly underlined its role with respect to reputational risk and opportunity, and good governance.

Note the consistent recurrence of reference to mutuality. Although this is invoked in slightly different ways, I take it to mean all parties having respect and understanding for others' points of view and working together to increase that respect and understanding. Of course, any organization may interact with two or more publics that disagree vehemently between themselves, meaning that the organization cannot be reconciled to all publics. Mutuality, however, doesn't require reconciliation, but rather continued dialogue with the intent to understand and be understood.

Such emphasis on mutuality is core to the fourth model. And in words from Chapter 1 of the book summing up the findings of Grunig *et al.*'s *Excellence* study: 'As a result of good public relations, both management and publics should behave in ways that minimize conflict or manage conflict effectively.'[27]

Two-way symmetric public relations relies on honest and open two-way communication and mutual give-and-take rather than one-way or asymmetric persuasion. It requires a management philosophy that recognizes that no organization stands alone but must instead adjust and adapt what it does and how it does it in order to align itself with its publics on the basis that this can only help not hinder the organization to achieve its objectives.

The *Cluetrain Manifesto* was the right way to say the right things at the right time, but it appears that its authors took their lead in part from the two-way symmetrical model and Patrick Jackson's compelling ability to convey the theory in practical terms in the *pr reporter* newsletter and other media. And they, in turn, on the prior perspectives of Edward Bernays[28] (the original PT Barnum style publicist) and Albert Sullivan[29] in the 1950s and 1960s.

For his part in asserting how his models apply in the digital age, Grunig re-endorses the two-way symmetrical model.[30]

It's worth then finishing this section on public relations with an extract from the preface of the *Excellence* book.[31] This concluded the *Excellence* team's 15 years of study, so I take its findings seriously:

> In a nutshell, we show that the value of public relations comes from the relationships that communicators develop and maintain with publics. We show that reputation is a product of relationships and that the quality of relationships and reputation result more from the behav-

ior of the organization than from the messages that communicators disseminate. We show that public relations can affect management decisions and behavior if it is headed by a manager who is empowered to play an essential role in the strategic management of the organization. In that role, communicators have their greatest value when they bring information into the organization, more than when they disseminate information out of the organization . . .

We show that communicators can develop relationships more effectively when they communicate symmetrically with publics rather than asymmetrically.

So there we have it. The definitions of marketing and PR are contentious. They vary, overlap and contradict. These are not exactly ideal foundations on which to move forward, but as this isn't a philosophical treatise we don't require ideals; it's only important that we understand the current landscape. To complete the picture, and this chapter, let's take a look at the phrase that's used to describe how all this is supposed to come together.

Integrated marketing communications

Integrated Marketing Communications: Putting it Together and Making it Work[32] by Don Schultz, Stanley Tannenbaum and Robert Lauterborn, is considered to be the seminal text on the subject. The authors have this to say in the 1993 book's introduction:

It's a new way of looking at the whole, where once we only saw parts such as advertising, public relations, sales promotion, purchasing, employee communications, and so forth. It's realigning communications to look at it the way the customer sees it – as a flow of information from indistinguishable sources. Professional communicators have always been condescendingly amused that consumers called everything 'advertising' or 'PR'. Now they recognize with concern if not chagrin that that's exactly the point – it is all one thing, at least to the consumer who sees or hears it.

The introduction proceeds to identify other traits of Integrated Marketing Communications (IMC) such as the need to elicit a response rather than just conduct a monologue, and accountability for results and outcomes, not just outputs. In particular it illuminates IMC's dedication to identifying and calculating ROI.

Don Schultz is Professor Emeritus-in-Service of Integrated Marketing Communication at Northwestern University's Medill School[33]. The School publishes the *Journal of Integrated Marketing Communications* (IMC), which at the time of writing defines IMC as:

> . . . a customer-centric, data-driven method of communicating with consumers. IMC – the management of all organized communications to build positive relationships with customers and other stakeholders – stresses marketing to the individual by understanding needs, motivations, attitudes and behaviors.
>
> . . . IMC not only integrates the marketing communications disciplines of advertising, direct and e-commerce marketing and public relations, but also advocates the alignment of all of a company's business processes, from product development to customer service.

Later, as we build our influence framework here, I'll be comparing and contrasting the framework with the vision of IMC as described in the later book by Schultz and Schultz, *IMC – The Next Generation: Five steps for delivering value and measuring returns using marketing communications.*[34] Coming a decade after Schultz's first book on the subject, it incorporates and adapts to the management theory, experience and technological innovations of the 90s and the early part of this century. This includes a move away from the original emphasis on what the seller wants to communicate to the consumer (outbound) towards a more reciprocal form of communication (outbound and inbound), and moving from an organization-centric to customer-centric focus.

The book adopts the definition of IMC employed by a study initiated in 1997 by the American Productivity and Quality Center (APQC)[35,36]:

> Integrated marketing communication is a strategic business process used to plan, develop, create, and evaluate coordinated, measurable, persuasive brand communication programs over time, with consumers, customers, prospects, and other targeted, relevant external and internal audiences.

As you'd expect, the book is a well-articulated and argued insight into the vision of ICM, and while you don't have to read it to make sense of this book, I do recommend it.

As Grunig defines the asymmetric model in terms of persuasion, I find the reference to persuasion in the APQC definition slightly incongruous with the claim to have moved away from a sole focus on outbound communications towards integration of both outbound and inbound. You can conduct persuasive communications and symmetric conversations concurrently, but the latter is not represented in the definition. Moreover, the book includes an organization chart with public relations reporting into the 'marcom manager', and a case study organization chart in which PR is listed under brand marketing.

The *Excellence* study honed in on IMC as you'd expect, attributing the matter sufficient gravitas to feature in the book's Preface. The *Excellence* findings show that excellent public relations functions are integrated, but not through another management function. 'We found that integrated marketing communication (IMC) is integrated into the integrated public relations function. IMC should not be the concept that integrates communication [PR].' Perhaps such concern is validated by the way the IMC book positions PR.

But let's drop back into the real world for a moment. I surveyed readers of my blog for their definition and regard for IMC,[37] and here are a couple of responses I thought most pertinent here.

Justin Hayward, Communications and Business Development Director of Telnic, has a go at cracking it in one punchy, slightly unusual and thought-provoking sentence that edges ahead of typical aspirations in my opinion:

> The product is the message is the experience is the feedback is the fanbase is the developer [product development] team.

Stephen Waddington, Managing Director of Speed Communications and highly regarded blogger on all aspects of public relations and marketing, speaks about IMC from the heart:

> It's a nonsense phrase. You wouldn't say let's use an integrated business approach would you? Yet the very fact we do use the term suggests that integrating marketing with other areas of the business is the exception rather than the norm. Marketing and PR should be connected to other areas of a business, but, try as hard as we might here at Speed, we know they aren't.

So thanks to Stephen for capturing, in four-dozen succinct words, one of the reasons I wanted to write this book. IMC is at once an important vision and too often a disappointing experience.

Summary

- Social, technological, environmental, legal and economic factors have demanded change to the way we go about marketing and PR
- The *Cluetrain Manifesto* and *Permission Marketing* signalled the cusp of this change in 1999
- Advertising has, possibly, come under the most pressure
- Experts don't agree on what precisely marketing and public relations are, let alone how they should co-exist.

We're now going to see if we can bring some clarity to this situation by stripping it back and asking ourselves: What exactly are we trying to achieve here?

2

As I am not an academic, I'm not presenting an academic paper. Moreover, there appears to be widespread recognition of a substantial gulf between academe and practitioners in both marketing and public relations disciplines, and you could say the two need to achieve some more two-way symmetrical communication.

Following the previous chapter's look at where we find ourselves today, this chapter begins a rethink. Fundamentally, I'm interested in finding ways for organizations to perform better – to improve the consistency with which they delight, and learn from, their stakeholders to the advantage of pursuing the vision.

I'm hoping this book might provide food for thought for those reviewing the organizational structure and integration of the traditional marketing and PR silos, and the capabilities demanded of those employed in these and associated disciplines.

A clean sheet

Let's take a clean sheet of paper and reconsider what all this marketing and PR business is intended to achieve. Fundamentally, what are we trying to do? And on the basis that the words and phrases that come with the 'baggage' of historic and current use and misuse are likely to confuse or narrow our thinking, can we articulate what we're trying to do without using such words as 'advertising', 'publicity', 'promotion', 'marketing', 'comms' and 'public relations'?

Such carte blanche thinking requires that each step be rational, and tidy definitions must be provided where ambiguity may otherwise muddy our intentions; we've already seen how important definitions can be, given that language, or at least our command and understanding of it, isn't perfect. There should be little need in my opinion for verbosity or extensive argument; it should make sense if it's to be really useful.

Some definitions

Let's start with some nouns and brief definitions. First we have 'organization' as there isn't much sense to this topic without it, and then descriptions of parties that surround it:

- *Organization* – an organized group of people with a particular purpose
- *Stakeholder* – a person or organization with an interest or concern in our organization or something our organization is involved in
- *Competitor* – an organization with objectives that clash with our own either directly (e.g. fly with us not them) or indirectly (e.g. don't fly, video conference instead).

Taking a step down into 'organization' we find:

- *For-profit* – primary motivation is to make and distribute surplus funds to owners
- *Non-profit* – primary motivation is not financial but to achieve some other ends; have a controlling board rather than owners
- *Public* – primary motivation set by the state and under the operational control of the state.

And, as it has appeared three times above:

- *Motivation* – reason(s) for acting or behaving in a particular way.

Taking a step down into 'stakeholder' we find the normal array:

- *Customer* – a person or organization that buys goods or services (where 'buys' includes paying with one's attention or time, and includes 'consumer').
- *Prospect* – a person or organization regarded as a potential customer

- *Client* – a person or organization under the care of another
- *Partner* – a person or company of importance to an organization in achieving its objectives (e.g. supplier, reseller, retailer)
- *Citizen* – a legally recognized subject or national of a state or commonwealth with rightful interest or concern in the workings of that nation or state
- *Employee* – a person employed for wages or salary (taken to include their dependents, and also retired employees still financially reliant upon the organization's ongoing success)
- *Shareholder* – an owner of shares in a for-profit organization (taken to include those with other financial holdings or investments contingent upon the organization's financial success).

You might say that the definition of stakeholder here could include competitors, but we'll adopt the common distinction between the two. Sometimes the stakeholder chooses to be a stakeholder (e.g., customer, employee). Sometimes the organization chooses stakeholders (e.g., partner, employee). And sometimes a stakeholder is a stakeholder by default (e.g., the citizen has to live somewhere).

Some include the environment and non-human sentient beings as stakeholders. I'm no utilitarian philosopher, so for our context here I'll regard citizens as taking representation by proxy.

Perhaps it's so obvious that it's not worth saying, but for the sake of completeness: No organization is an island. Rather, it must interact with all those parties around it in order to pursue and achieve its objectives, and the nature of its interactions is or should be defined and governed by its motivation and objectives and the strategies formed to achieve its objectives (something we look at in more detail in the next chapter).

Mapping the interactions

Now we can begin to map out the interactions based on this *Oxford English Dictionary* definition:

- *Interaction* – reciprocal action or influence.

Working with our definitions of organization, stakeholders and competitors, we have four primary types of interactions:

1. The interactions between our organization and stakeholders
2. The interactions between our stakeholders with respect to us
3. The interactions between our competitors and stakeholders
4. The interactions between stakeholders with respect to our competitors.

I refer to these as primary interactions because one could also look at the interaction between our organization and competitors in, for example, so-called coopetition (cooperative competition), or trade association activities. One could also look at the interactions of our stakeholders with the competition's stakeholders where they are exclusive of each other, such as those between football fans of opposing teams. I found however that, while these may be important interactions, they didn't have a material impact on this rethink, and the resultant model works to encompass these interactions accordingly.

Mapping the influence flows

We can break down interaction (reciprocal action) into action one way and action the other way. Or indeed the influence one way and the influence the other way, where the verb influence is defined as:

- *Influence* – to have an effect on the character, development, or behaviour of someone or something.

In other words, you have been influenced when you think in a way you wouldn't otherwise have thought, or do something you wouldn't otherwise have done.

This gives us six primary influence flows:

1. Our organization's influence with stakeholders
2. Our stakeholders' influence with each other with respect to us
3. Our stakeholders' influence with our organization
4. Our competitors' influence with stakeholders

5. Stakeholders' influence with each other with respect to our competitors

6. Stakeholders' influence with our competitors.

(I liked the term 'influence flow' when I first started to use it. It was only upon writing this chapter that I discovered that the word 'influence' itself originates from medieval Latin '*influentia*', meaning 'in-flow'. I hope, then, that you'll excuse any remaining tautology.)

Figure 2.1 portrays these flows. For simplicity, I have lumped all stakeholders in the middle but, of course, our organization and our competitors may not share a universal set of stakeholders.

We have started to fill in our blank sheet. We have now crafted a simple framework on which we can continue to build, particularly looking more at the nature of those arrows, but for the sake of keeping it connected to real life as we know it today, let's take some time out and do just that.

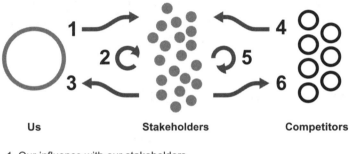

Us   **Stakeholders**   **Competitors**

1. Our influence with our stakeholders
2. Our stakeholders' influence with each other in respect to us
3. Our stakeholders' influence with us
4. Our competitors' influence with our stakeholders
5. Our stakeholders' influence with each other in respect to our competitors
6. Our stakeholders' influence with our competition

Figure 2.1: The Six Influence Flows

Contrasting the six influence flows with the traditional emphases

It's probably too simplistic but not too far off the mark to consider the historic focus of marketing and PR practice as being predominantly on the 1st influence flow (our influence with our stakeholders), with a bit of the 3rd in the form of the internal circulation of news clippings for example, and eliciting information with marketing research to improve one's understanding of consumer preferences, attitudes, and behaviours (as long as you systematically ensure that these have an influence, of course).

Sometimes we also try to infer a 3rd flow (our stakeholders' influence with us) from implicit data such as sales volume or growth – 'it's not selling as fast as we'd expected, there must be something they don't like.'

Should a competitor have great success with their 1st flow (the competitor's 1st flow is our 4th) then one might conduct some ad hoc research to find out how it acted upon stakeholders.

This traditional emphasis was probably down to a combination of what appeared to work at the time, what was expected at the time, and what was possible within the systematic and budget constraints of your typical marketing and PR operation. In my experience, too few marketing and PR teams have solid research capabilities, but this itself is an effect, not a cause – an effect of organizations' inability to optimize resource to best meet the business objectives, but more on that later.

The 2nd flow and the Internet

The first three PR models focus on the 1st influence flow, our influence with our stakeholders. Even where the two-way symmetrical model for PR is adopted (honest and open two-way communication and mutual give-and-take), the emphasis remains on treating the 1st and 3rd influence flows equally. Or does it? What about the 2nd flow (our stakeholders' influence with each other in respect to us)?

I mentioned earlier that Grunig continues to support the validity of the two-way symmetrical model in the digital age and in *Paradigms of Global Public Relations in the Age of Digitalization*,[38] he specifically responds to quotes from two books: 'The Web has changed everything', according to Brian Solis and Deirdre Breakenridge in *Putting the Public back in Public Relations: How Social Media is Reinventing the Aging Business of PR*[39]; and '. . . it is hard to avoid making the claim that 'the internet changes everything' . . . for public relations the unavoidable conclusion is that nothing will ever be the same again', from David Phillips and Philip Young in *Online Public Relations: A Practical Guide to Developing an Online Strategy in the World of Social Media.*[40] They continue:

> [The] Excellence [study] characterizes the vector of communication as being between an organization and its publics, and is concerned with the balance – the symmetry – of this transaction. The bold claim that emerges from the arguments put forward for 'the new PR' is that the fundamental vector of communication that shapes reputation and an organization's relationship with its stakeholders has flipped through 90 degrees Now, the truly significant discourse is that which surrounds an organization, product or service, a conversation that is enabled and given form and substance by the interlinked, aggregated messages that emerge from internet mediated social networks.[41]

This quote is, in our framework here, asserting that 'new PR' has the 1st and 3rd influence flows subservient to the 2nd.

Grunig responds to the claims the Internet changes everything:

> In one sense, I agree with these assertions. For most practitioners, digital media do change everything about the way they practice public relations. Other practitioners, however, doggedly use the new media in the same way that they used traditional media. From a theoretical per-spective, in addition, I do not believe digital media change the public relations theory needed to guide practice, especially our generic princi-ples of public relations. Rather, the new media facilitate the application of the principles and, in the future, will make it difficult for practition-ers around the world not to use the principles.

And to the claim by Phillips and Young that things have 'flipped through 90 degrees':

> In contrast, I do not believe that the 'internet society' or the 'new PR' challenges the Excellence paradigm, as Phillips and Young argued in these two passages. They seem to believe that 'an organization and its publics' are distinct from 'internet-mediated social networks'. Instead,

> I believe that an organization and its publics now are embedded in internet-mediated social networks but that public relations is still about an organization's relationships with its publics. Organizations do not need relationships with individuals who are not members of their publics even though these people might be actively communicating with and building relationships with each other. Organizations simply do not have the time or resources to cultivate relationships with everyone – only with individuals or groups who have stakes in organizations because of consequences that publics or organizations have or might have on each other.

I think Phillips and Young have a point, although perhaps not justified quite as I will do now, and Grunig may have missed another. Both have practical ramifications.

First, 'Internet-mediated' communication isn't just a new media form in my opinion. It has unprecedented emergent behaviour, a scientific term used to describe how very many relatively simple interactions (e.g. blogging, tweeting, sharing) can give rise to complex systems[42] – systems that exhibit one or more properties as a whole that aren't manifest for smaller parts or individual components. The weather is a complex system, for example. Returning from meteorology to marketing, if you have ever asked yourself something along the lines of 'How come this 'went viral' and that one didn't?', then you have contemplated the influence of a complex system.

By definition, this behaviour cannot be attributed to one or a set of relationships with one or a set of stakeholders. It is the combination of the whole that itself exerts influence. You can't learn about termite mounds from studying the individual termite. Put simply, it's in the mix, and we'll return to complex systems later.

Secondly, what are these 'relationships' to which Grunig refers? This is obviously central to Grunig's paradigm, given that 'relations' is the R in PR.

- *Relationship* – the way in which two or more people or things are connected, or the state of being connected.

But with our blank sheet approach we have freed ourselves from such constructs, and all we have are Six Influence Flows that may or may not be based on 'relationships' with 'publics'. I said earlier that Grunig *may* have missed this, but he hasn't in terms of the world as viewed through a public relations lens; it's just that we've laid all the lenses down.

So instead of saying that 'organizations do not need relationships with individuals who are not members of their publics', we can say that organizations will find it advantageous to maintain awareness of all Six Influence Flows regardless of the genesis or properties of the influence that flows therein. Organizations can prepare for the expected and unexpected emergence of influences that might warrant attention, because perhaps they represent reputational risk, or an opportunity for organizational learning, or a positive sentiment that can be harnessed in constructive ways.

A new stakeholder

Perhaps we have also found a new stakeholder in our framework, an individual who did not know she was a stakeholder until . . . hang on there, look, she just shared that link. And she also added a little comment. Atoms of influence.

She is the modern manifestation of the *netizen*, a term coined by Michael Hauben in 1992 and described by him in the preface to a book by the IEEE on the topic[43]:

> These people understand the value of collective work and the communal aspects of public communications. These are the people who discuss and debate topics in a constructive manner, who e-mail answers to people and provide help to new-comers, who maintain FAQ files and other public information repositories, who maintain mailing lists, and so on. These are people who discuss the nature and role of this new communications medium. These are the people who act as citizens of the Net.

This new stakeholder requires clear differentiation from the others in order to be relevant here. Netizens are not 'online publics' in the normal 'digital PR' context; such groups are simply the usual stakeholders with Internet access. Rather, netizens are stakeholders *because* they are online and *because* they are willing to act in ways that represent their moral compass so to speak – their feelings for what is right and wrong, or good and bad. Or perhaps they act simply on what makes them happy or sad, excited or chillaxed. The netizen is a most complex being whose responses boil down to a synaptic-like mouse click, or not. And given that humans are unchanged, some act apparently rationally, others have no regard for logical discourse whatsoever, and the majority lie somewhere in between.

And there are many many millions of them.

So instead of Grunig saying 'organizations simply do not have the time or resources to cultivate relationships with everyone', we can say that organizations will find it advantageous to wield information technologies to 'relate' to the use (both directly and programmatically) of information technologies by others.

Summary

- No organization is an island
- The Six Influence Flows is a new and simple model to think about what we're trying to achieve
- The 1st flow (our influence with our stakeholders) and 3rd flow (our stakeholders' influence with us) are well understood, even if the 3rd is rarely attributed symmetrical/equal importance with the 1st
- The 2nd flow (our stakeholders' influence with each other with respect to us) has caused debate in the context of previously accepted models
- 'Internet mediated' communication exhibits emergent behaviour
- Organizations will find it advantageous to maintain awareness of all Six Influence Flows regardless of the genesis or properties of the influence that flows therein
- The netizen is a new stakeholder – not synonymous with 'online publics' but rather a person who responds to stimuli online
- Organizations will find it advantageous to wield information technologies to 'relate' to the use (both directly and programmatically) of information technologies by others.

Given that we're pivoting our model here on influence, we're going to invest the next chapter looking more deeply into what we mean by the word and how it relates to many of the other words and phrases in common use.

3

This short chapter continues to tease out the language to ensure that we're all singing with the same hymn sheet. I'm afraid there's no getting around the need for such diligence – we've already seen how fuzzy terminology and past casual (mis)use of words has led to contradiction and befuddlement.

To me, influence is our be all and end all here. A quick reminder: you have been influenced when you think in a way you wouldn't otherwise have thought, or do something you wouldn't otherwise have done.

We can rephrase the Six Influence Flows:

1. Are we having the appropriate influence?
2. What influence do the stakeholders have on each other about us?
3. Are stakeholders appropriately influencing us?
4. How are our competitors influencing stakeholders?
5. What influence do the stakeholders have on each other about our competitors?
6. Are stakeholders appropriately influencing our competitors?

Influence, however, is a word that is just moving into that danger zone where it acquires some of the baggage we were trying to leave behind. During 2010 we witnessed marketing and PR practitioners develop an increasing obsession with various social networking number-crunching services positioned as being able to divine who's got it; influence.

The problem with such services is their confusing popularity for influence. One can only determine that influence has taken place when you know someone now thinks in a way they wouldn't otherwise have thought, or did something they wouldn't otherwise have done. Brian Solis's August 2010 blog post, *Please Repeat: Influence is not Popularity*,[44] does a super job of teasing this out, and my presentation on the subject to the Monitoring Social Media Bootcamp in London during March 2010 left no one in the audience confused as to how I rate such specious popularity-oriented measures.[45]

In *Influencer Grudge Match: Lady Gaga versus Bono – What Makes an Influencer?*,[46] a white paper co-authored by Brian Solis and Frank Strong, the number one finding illuminates the confusion:

> Influence is different from popularity . . . An overwhelming 90% of respondents perceive a big difference between 'influence' and 'popularity'. However, qualitative review of open-ended comments on this question shows the distinction is not always clear. A follow-on question also adds ambiguity, with 84% of respondents saying that there is a correlation between 'reach' and 'influence' on social networks.

We return to this issue later in the section 'No standard for influence' in Chapter 5.

The greatest risk for misinterpretation here, however, comes with the use of the word in the sole context of the exertion of influence to the exclusion of the reciprocal. The word 'influence' can carry negative connotations when it is viewed in terms of persuasion (what the PR theorists would refer to as the intent of the 3rd (asymmetric) model, and what marketers in general might refer to as manipulation, including the less than scrupulous variety).

But our framework here has no need for such slants or devices. It simply pivots on the activity in all directions that causes minds to be changed and actions to alter. And unless stated otherwise, I always use the word 'influence' in this book to mean all six flows.

Some pundits consider influence to be one of a range of activities or factors.

For example, Brian Solis presents a 'formula' for social media activities: 'relevance + resonance = significance'.[47] He then defines online significance as 'the culmination of reputation, trust, influence, accessibility, value, and capital within each social network', even though concepts such as reputation, influence or accessibility don't feature in his definitions of relevance and resonance. Somewhat confusingly, he also defines resonance as a function of relevance.

I think perhaps I'm analysing it all a little too literally with a mathematician's head in a way that Brian didn't intend to accommodate. Moreover, he may treat his blog as I treat mine – a place to try things out. Nevertheless, I structure it slightly differently and such a structure is important in considering whether the framework we develop in this book is fit for purpose or an oversimplification: whether influence is indeed the be all and end all.

Some definitions first:

- *Relevance* – closely connected or appropriate to the matter in hand
- *Resonance* – the power to evoke enduring images, memories, and emotions
- *Accessible* – easily understood or appreciated; friendly and easy to talk to; approachable
- *Reputation* – the beliefs or opinions that are generally held about someone or something
- *Trust* – firm belief in the reliability, truth or ability of someone or something
- *Significance* – the quality of being worthy of attention: importance.

We can look at this list as two halves.

- *The first half* – Relevance, resonance and accessibility are all qualities that stakeholders might form about us over a relatively short period based on how effectively we go about influencing and being influenced. They might watch a video we posted on YouTube, or grab a sales brochure from a shop, or discuss our brand with their mates and find it relevant to their needs or desires. They might post something about one of our brands, or leave a voice-mail for the procurement team and revel when we respond, concluding that we are indeed accessible.
- *The second half* – Our behaviours, manifest in influencing and being influenced through products and services and policies and customer relations and communications and interactions of all kinds, accumulate over a longer period to form a reputation and a degree of trustworthiness in people's minds, and to establish a level of significance in people's lives. This cannot

be achieved in the 42 seconds of a YouTube video or an hour in a show-room. It's more of a long-term, sedimentary process.

The task at hand is influence. The resulting perception in the first instance may be described in terms of relevance, resonance and accessibility. The outcomes in the longer term are reputation, trust and significance. Along the way we're also aiming to attract purchases and expressions of preference and recommendation, or any other manifestation of thought or action we're hoping to secure; and greater insight into, and articulation of, our stakeholders' situations, needs and desires to help to decide what we want to do and how we want to do it.

Not that we use the terms in our framework here, but reputation management does not actually mean managing reputation, and brand management does not actually mean managing a brand. They mean actively attending to the business of influencing and being influenced such that the resultant beliefs or opinions held about us and our products are conducive to our achieving organizational objectives.

Similarly, when Chris Lake, Econsultancy's Director of Innovation, writes: 'It's all about engagement',[48] and when Katie Delahaye Paine asserts in her presentation *Are We Engaged Yet?*: 'The definition of success has changed – The answer isn't how many you've reached, but how those you've reached have responded',[49] they are emphasizing engagement as a measurable outcome of influence.

- *Engage* – occupy or attract someone's interest or attention; involve someone in a conversation or discussion.

Table 3.1 sums this up.

Table 3.1: Example shorter- and longer-term manifestations of influence

Shorter-term	Longer-term
Relevance	Reputation
Resonance	Trust
Accessibility	Significance
Engagement	Authenticity
Curiosity	Authority

I've concluded then that this influence framework is beautifully simple without need for the allowances and exceptions that oversimplifications demand.

Summary

- You have been influenced when you think in a way you wouldn't otherwise have thought, or do something you wouldn't otherwise have done
- Influence is not popularity
- Our framework pivots on the activity in all directions that causes minds to be changed and actions to alter
- The influence framework covers all bases without redundancy.

In the next chapter, we review the facets of the social Web and social Web analytics.

4

You'll know by now that I like to make sure we're all using words and phrases in the same way, which I hope you'll agree is useful, and with that intention in mind let me break down how I use 'social Web' differently to 'social media'.

Social media is a term that describes all the media that aren't traditional media, and by traditional media I refer to what some call 'industrial' and others call 'mass' media; stuff that's designed, procured and waved under your nose by a company aiming to meet a consumer need (and, usually, sell some space to advertisers along the way).

Social media enable consumers to be producers. Or, more precisely, it's media where the organization that facilitates the media allows the public to interact with each other, pivoting around relationships, points of view and/or content (except, of course, where the organization hosting the conversation sells some space to advertisers along the way). The media organization may stimulate the conversation, via the original publication of news and editorial for example, but the peer-to-peer debate can then proceed, and often with zest.

I see social media as a component of the social Web, where the social Web consists of:

1. *Social media* – For example: Facebook, Ping, blogs, Twitter, Flickr, YouTube, Amazon customer reviews, debate at *The Guardian* and *USA Today*, and social news at Slashdot and Digg
2. *Applications* – For example: Outlook, Wordpress, Tweetdeck, social news apps such as Flipboard and My Taptu,[50] the Facebook app, Foursquare and Gowalla, iTunes, Spotify, social network and contact information tools

such as LinkedIn toolbars and Xobni, instant messenger, Skype, social commerce applications such as Shopkick and Blippy, and socially sourced augmented reality with applications such as Layar

3. *Services* – For example: email, Delicious and StumbleUpon social book-marking, friend location information from Foursquare and Facebook Places, socially augmented search, and social commerce services such as Swipely

4. *The network of devices* – Desktops, laptops, phones, tablets and netbooks, and potentially anything we interact with (see 'Mobile and other things' in Chapter 8).

Before we dive into social Web analytics, four quick asides spring to mind that help to lend colour to this conversation.

You'll have noticed that some products and services span two or more of these 'layers' of the social Web, and perhaps therein lies both flexibility and strength; it certainly describes the apparent determinations of Apple, Google and Facebook.

It's worth noting that the distinction of *social* media and *social* Web will likely go the way of *colour* TV, dropping the 'social' part as the social component becomes pervasive and defaults. I propose the same for *digital* marketing in the digital marketing chapter of the CIM's centenary celebration book, The Marketing Century.[51]

We discussed earlier how the social Web is a complex system demonstrating emergent behaviours with respect to the influence that emergence might exert; and it now seems that the mechanics of the social Web itself also show signs of evolving in that way. I recall my fascination, for example, for the way in which retweeting emerged mid-2008 to the point where I was conscious of my first retweet being not just an endorsement of the person whose tweet I was retweeting but of the idea and syntax of retweeting itself. There was no edict from Twitter. This was no prescribed behaviour. It just emerged.

Influence flows are 'platform agnostic'. Just like water, if there's a way to flow, it will flow that way. It is incumbent on influence professionals to understand that and deal with it. Your influence strategy will guide your approach in each instance, but each instance does not have its own strategy.

There is then no such thing in my book as a Twitter strategy or a Facebook strategy; these are channels requiring tactical management in line with your marketing or PR strategy,[52] or, more widely, what we refer to here as the influence strategy.

Social Web analytics

Like many, I consider the social Web to be one of the most exciting developments in social, cultural, political and commercial history. I can empathize with any leadership team of any type of organization should they have considered the social Web to be an immense and fearsome creature. Their landscape for public stakeholder expression went in a relatively short space of time from consisting of the press and the occasional 'letter to the editor' to millions of public conversations; with all expressions not only everlasting but also everlastingly accessible. Organizations need help to keep track of it all.

Social Web analytics is the application of search, indexing, semantic analysis and business intelligence technologies to the task of identifying, tracking, listening to and participating in the distributed conversations about a particular brand, product or issue, with emphasis on quantifying the trend in each conversation's sentiment and influence.

At least, that is the definition I used, and still stand by, in my Social Web Analytics eBook 2008[53] (although perhaps 'conversation' is too narrow in future, as we'll see later). I'll quote part of my ebook's Preface here to lend some context:

> If you could go back to the mid-90s and offer a marketer a little box that could sit on her desk and let her listen in on thousands of customer conversations and participate in those discussions regardless of geography or time zone, it would appear so far-fetched that she'd probably call security. This ebook is about that reality.

Published mid-2008, the first half of the ebook recorded the beginnings of an incredible technology and expanded on how this might all develop. The second half described some of the earliest players. My list of a dozen or so analytics services in the ebook had expanded five-fold within a year, and Nathan Gilliatt was tracking in excess of 200 related services at one point.[54] This explosion – given the time it would take to analyse such a number in any useful detail – explains why I didn't write a follow-up.

I believe it was Forrester who popularized the term 'listening platform' in 2009. 'Monitoring tools' is another oft-used phrase, as is 'social media analytics'. I'm not enamoured of Altimeter Group's use of the label 'social marketing analytics',[55] which appears to imply that public relations is a subset of marketing and that all the conversations under analysis here are the result of marketing activities.

I'll stick with 'social Web analytics' for good reasons. Firstly, analysis entails listening and much more, such as making operationally useful sense of the data. When David Meerman Scott included my definition in his 2010 book *Real-Time Marketing & PR*,[56] he followed it immediately with his reaction:

> Wow. That's a mouthful! But read it again slowly and it will start to make sense. This is more than just monitoring what people say. Indeed, some organizations are becoming extremely sophisticated in their use of various available tools.

Secondly, social Web analytics refers to the social Web and not just social media, and I imagined that such services would need to expand their scope to include applications, services and the network itself at some juncture to remain relevant. (We'll explore that further later.) Thirdly, unlike the Altimeter Group's term, it doesn't infer any origin of the conversation under analysis. And lastly, I like the connection the phrase has with good old-fashioned (if any discipline still in its teenage years can be called old-fashioned) Web analytics – the measurement, collection, analysis and reporting of data associated with the delivery and use of one's own website.

The Web Analytics Association has recently evolved the definition of Web analytics to cover both what's described as on-site and off-site. On-site is the self-explanatory traditional definition of the Web analytics' domain, and the addition of off-site is intended to cover social Web analytics.[57] If I have asserted above that we may drop the *social* of *social* media at some juncture, then perhaps we should do the same for *social* Web analytics.

Characteristics of social Web analytics services

Michael Brewer proposes eight categories in his January 2010 ebook, *Listening Platforms – Competitive Landscape*[58]:

1. Wide scope analytical and reporting tools for all aspects of marketing and customer management
2. Blog-based influencing tools, designed to gain access to influential customers / commentators
3. PR and media management tools for reputation management and opinion-forming influence
4. Social media tracking and intervention
5. Fraud protection, security and threat detection
6. News media tracking
7. Social media within sales management
8. Tools that bring social media alongside other customer communications tracking.

I include this list here because it's a succinct way to communicate the manner in which social Web analytics can be put to use, but I don't believe that any such stratification has really existed concretely – and nor is it likely to. Brewer himself adds: 'Category 1 is the most comprehensive. All tools may head towards this category over time.'

Now is not the time to detail my thoughts on how this market will evolve, but in summary we'll see consolidation, specialism (in components of the service), vertical integration, horizontal integration and the emergence of a standardized method to structure data representing an 'atom of influence' for data portability.[59]

As it is still a relatively nascent industry, social Web analytics services vary widely, so let's run through 12 primary characteristics that will inform your choice of service or allow you to review the suitability of your current services. We're investing this time because you can't expect to keep track of the

Six Influence Flows without a mature understanding and application of these services.

1. Breadth of indexing/languages

Breadth of indexing describes the range of content the service aims to find and catalogue against which you can run your search criteria. This can be as narrow as 'just Twitter', or as wide as 200 million forums, blogs, social networks and other websites across 40 different languages. Not that quantity always trumps quality, of course – for example, a service that prides itself on indexing Danish language blogs may be just what you need if your product is designed specifically for the Danish-speaking market.

Does the service provider repeatedly visit all the websites, or does it acquire the content from a third party that does the visiting and indexing? You might not care, but a service that does it itself may be more amenable to any suggestions you propose concerning its list of sources than it would if it relied solely on intermediaries.

Also under the heading of breadth of indexing is the service's approach to de-duplication, or 'de-duping' for short. Content syndication is widespread, so you will want to know if a particular service de-dupes such replication, whether it is grouped for you to see how one piece of content is syndicated, or whether it makes no attempt at de-duping. Given that each instance might spark its own conversation, grouped analysis might be preferable.

2. Multimedia indexing

The primary focus of social analytics today is the written word, yet the Web is becoming an increasingly multimedia experience. Depending on your specific needs relating to your brand, product and marketplace, you may wish to find services that can index and interpret audio and video content. This remains a very difficult task, as I'm sure you can appreciate, but various companies are working hard to improve accuracy and reliability. (If you are publishing audio and video content presently, consider the addition of a transcript to make it much easier to find.)

3. Rate of indexing

Sparked by Twitter, the so-called 'real-time Web' went big in 2009 when Bing, and then Google, entered the game during the second half of the year. This is manifest on Google by the 'Updates' link to its search results pages and on Bing by 'Social' (you might need to find it under 'More' on both).

The real-time Web places a much higher value on very recent contributions to the social Web – that is, in minutes or seconds ago rather than hours or days. It's apparent in different ways for blogging and micro-blogging (Twitter). Ask yourself how far into a stream of comments on a blog post you typically dive; do you get to the tenth comment, let alone the tenth page of comments? In other words, the earlier the comment (i.e. the shorter the time lapse between the post being published and the response) the more attention it commands. With Twitter, the conversational thread is very easy to lose if the lag between a tweet and a response is measured in hours, and often a fraction of an hour is sufficient to disrupt the flow.

The rate of indexing is therefore increasingly important for the noisiest markets. Notification of a relevant post by an influential blogger within 5 minutes of it going live is so much more valuable to you than a delay of hours if the post goes on to attract 10 comments an hour. If your market is quieter, or if, for example, the most important blogger in your space attracts comments at the rate of one a day, the rate of blog indexing isn't going to concern you very much.

4. Search query structure

How do you tell the social Web analytics service exactly what you are looking for? At its simplest, the social Web analytics service offers you the same as the Google homepage: a search box. A step up from this is analogous to Google's advanced search where you can be more specific about things such as phrases, exclusions, languages and dates. This is often fine for a quick analysis, for investigating a new business prospect or partner for example, or for informing a new product development brainstorm. Nevertheless, it will fit the bill better if your organization, its brands and those of your competitors have unique names (e.g. HSBC, Mozilla) rather than everyday or ambiguous names (e.g. Shell, Gap).

The other end of the spectrum is the search manager that is allocated to you by the social Web analytics vendor. Search managers are expert in their company's service, and is expert at working with you to construct detailed search queries that may run to pages and, critically, honing them regularly over time from the results that get returned. If your brand name consists of an everyday word and you operate in a very noisy market (e.g. Target, Orange, Creative), then you may well need some serious help in honing your search terms.

5. Semantic analysis and sentiment

Sentiment analysis is the part of semantic analysis that aims to determine the author's emotional regard for, or attitude towards, something from the text alone. Given the complexity involved, the output is often classified on a simple ordinal scale: e.g. negative, neutral and positive.

At present there is nothing like a perfect semantic analysis approach, and there is also considerable variation in capability. Humans are highly adept at understanding the context in which words are used, but software is less capable. Humans can infer meaning, but it is very difficult to program machines to do so. Humans can detect and deal with sarcasm and irony in a way that no semanticist has ever crystallized in software code.

You may read a critique of the latest HP Envy notebook that rates some features highly, notes the omission of one or two nice-to-haves, and bemoans the touchpad. You can weigh up in your mind whether this warms you towards the notebook or otherwise, but how should the social Web analytics service employed by HP's marketing and communications team rate the sentiment of this piece?

Some social Web analytics services don't employ semantic analysis at all. Rather, they may attempt to distinguish HP, the successful technology company, from the abbreviation for Horse Power by constructing more traditional search queries, looking for words like 'printer', 'PC' and 'camera' close to the reference to HP, and, equally, for the absence of references to 'car', 'motorbike' or 'engine'. But how will they cope if HP wheels an electric vehicle out of its Silicon Valley garage?

Tracking sentiment (sometimes referred to as tonality) over time helps you to establish whether things are going your way or not, and exactly how.

The service without a semantic analysis capability may allow you to determine the sentiment manually for each item it brings to your attention, and let you log your conclusion. (And most services with semantic analysis permit manual override.) Manual assessment could be sufficient for a few hundred mentions a month, but if your organization is likely to generate thousands or tens of thousands of mentions each month, this will soon prove ugly to scale.

To date, the most advanced services claim accuracy in some situations of up to 75% when compared to human analysis on a simple ordinal scale, but typically most hit their limits at around 65%. Giles Palmer, Managing Director Brandwatch, tells me that typically 65% of social Web contributions are neutral; that is, are neither complimentary nor derogatory. So just claiming all contributions to be neutral gets you to 65% accuracy.

Semantic analysis is costly to develop and costly to operate, so you can expect such functionality to come at a price. It's a critical criterion.

6. Influence and customer lifetime value

If your analytics service aims to highlight some social Web contributions over others – which is, of course, vital if your brand commands thousands of mentions a week – then sentiment is just one variable. You may want it to highlight the noisiest threads, and the more 'influential' sources over the less so. (See Chapter 5 on 'Measurement, complexity and influence-centricity' on this point.)

Quantifying someone's influence is difficult, as we discussed earlier, and there have been some weird and wonderful attempts to do so. Some approaches represent an interesting and useful estimate, while others appear to be simply misguided and/or misleading. If you intend to rely on a service's quantitative assessment of influence, then you will want to understand how it reaches its conclusions. If a vendor ignores your enquiry or if the response is vague, run Forest run.

Customer lifetime value (CLV) is another way to try to prioritize some conversations over others. It's an approach that has been carried over from customer relationship management (CRM) and its application here depends on your ability to link social Web profiles with customer records, which is rarely if ever an easily automated task and will most likely require your customers to declare their social Web usernames and handles. Remember however, as we'll briefly mention again later, that CLV focuses on the value of the customer herself and not the total value she might bring in recruiting new customers.

Some refer to the separation or prioritization of conversations as categorization.

7. Workflow

Your social Web strategy will inform your approach to workflow.

How exactly do you want to respond to the conversations highlighted to you by the analytics service? Are you assessing sentiment manually? How many people are part of the workflow and who has responsibility for replying? Do you want to allocate one person per conversation? Are responses managed through the service? If not, what other mechanism is there for tracking a particular conversation? What criteria identify a conversation as demanding immediate and urgent attention, perhaps by a rapidly convened response team? How are these criteria applied?

Is (near) real-time feedback to engineering or product development required, and if so how is this facilitated? Will the service integrate with existing customer service / help desk processes such as ticketing systems?

Some now refer to the influence, customer lifetime value, and workflow aspects as social customer relationship management (SCRM) or, recognizing that this process applies to all stakeholders and not only customers, social relationship management (SRM).

8. Reporting

Good-looking charts do not make a good social Web analytics service; it is much better to have great analysis and less attractive charts than the other way round. Of course, fabulous analysis and gorgeous charts would be lovely.

The approach to reporting has typically varied from having bespoke representations built into the service by the provider to their tailoring reporting software and extensions to sit 'in front' of their service. And, as we'll see later in the Balanced Scorecard section of this book, it will become increasingly common for an organization to want to output the information, such as overall status and management reports, to an existing corporate dashboarding system.

9. Integration, APIs and libraries

API stands for Application Programming Interface, and libraries in this context are repositories of code that can be called upon remotely as needed. Your longer-term integration of social Web analytics into other business systems (e.g. integration with your CRM system as mentioned earlier) may pivot on the availability of these items.

I like to refer to such integration as the ERPing of social Web analytics, where ERP is Enterprise Resource Planning – the term describing the large corporate systems from such organizations as SAP, Cisco and The Sage Group. You may be delighted to know, however, that further discussion of such details is beyond the scope of this book.

10. Applications, services and the network of devices

I referred earlier to the potential for such services to extend their scope beyond social media into applications, services and the network of devices: i.e. the whole social Web. The opportunities are manifold:

Applications

The data describing your customers' use of your smartphone app, including location-based data, or from your organization's work with third-party social commerce and augmented reality apps, can be pulled into your social Web analytics.

An obvious example today is scrobbling, which is a term that was originally coined by the last.fm service, but is now used more widely. Scrobbling involves logging the songs (or any digital content) you play on your media player for subsequent sharing with a service provider or others. Apple now takes full advantage of this capability with its iTunes application and Ping music social network.

Services

One example here is the tracking and analysis of user-curated social news streams to determine brand and topic association.

The network of devices

Consumer electronics companies are increasingly trying to track and analyse product use data, possibly subject to the user's opt-in (see 'Mobile and other things' in Chapter 8). Scrobbling, for example, may entail getting the play information from your mp3 player or other device. In the world of keep-fit and athletics, an iPod can record the distance and pace of a walk or run, either directly with the MotionX application or in conjunction with the Nike+ iPod training shoe sensor for subsequent uploading and sharing via iTunes.

11. Commercial and legal

What is the pricing structure? Per seat? Per search query? Per language? Annual? Pay-as-you-go? How does multi-campaign agency licensing work? Are there discounts for multiple campaign tracking? What's the service level agreement? How does the licensing address the copyright of the reports generated by the service and the material it collates? Are you indemnified for the use of their service for any claims made in relation to patent, copyright or trademark infringement?

12. Viability

Analytics forms an essential part of your business intelligence going forward, so you will want to ensure that your investment in time and money goes on a service that is supported by appropriate resources. While a service running today from its founder's bedroom could be the next big thing – and one of the well-funded vendors could always hit the wall – this market is now sufficiently mature for your normal due diligence in the procurement process to apply.

Moreover, this market is ripe for consolidation. You may have a preference to work with a vendor that is more likely to be doing the acquiring than being acquired, but that preference will be secondary to ensuring that you do not select a partner that does neither and is then squeezed out of the market. If such an outcome was to materialize, you will be faced with integrating a new service into your organizational systems and processes, re-zeroing your organization's trending key performance indicators, and retraining your staff in a new system with new terminology, new user interface and new report formats.

Achieving an 'Awesome Analytics Advantage'

We can take the idea of the ERPing of social Web analytics further.

Today, the databases underpinning social Web analytics, on-site Web analytics, CRM, retail analytics, service delivery and other operational aspects are often treated as silos and never, to my knowledge, wholly connected. The first influence professionals who work with their IT teams to forge ways to tie them together and begin to connect the data records in each database relating to the same stakeholder, will have what I describe with just a little tongue in cheek as an 'Awesome Analytics Advantage', or Triple-A for short. This adds a new dimension to traditional business intelligence (BI).

This task is far from easy but the prospect looked a little more attainable in 2010 as IBM and SAS, for example, entered the social Web analytics market – both of whom are serious players in the other databases and applications mentioned above and rather adept at making those connections.

Summary

- The social Web consists of social media, applications, services and the network of devices
- The social Web is one of the most exciting developments in social, cultural, political and commercial history

- Social Web analytics is the application of searching, indexing, semantic analysis and business intelligence technologies to the task of identifying, tracking, listening to and participating in the distributed conversations about a particular brand, product or issue, with emphasis on quantifying the trend in each conversation's sentiment and influence
- Being a nascent capability, social Web analytics services vary widely and each organization must appreciate its specific needs prior to procurement
- Connecting data records across various databases could deliver an 'Awesome Analytics Advantage'.

We have a new model, clarified what we mean by influence, and explored current social analytical capabilities. The next chapter takes us into measurement, complexity and what I refer to as influence-centricity. This will take us to the point that will allow us to proceed in later chapters to consider business performance management and the Balanced Scorecard, followed by the Influence Scorecard.

5

I find myself repeating one criticism too frequently: 'measurement because we can, not because we should'. This chapter is about aspiring to measure only what we should.

Measurement

I was never satisfied with common PR measurement approaches, or indeed with many other approaches to marketing measurement. They too often appear vague. Measurement and evaluation come across too frequently as more about post-rationalizing our decisions to pursue particular strategies and campaigns or proving to our clients that they should continue to retain us, than about seeking to secure an objective organizational learning opportunity.

Take the traditional reliance of the PR profession on advertising value equivalence (AVE); a greater waste of time and effort you couldn't hope to find. In all my years in PR I have always refused point blank to 'calculate' AVE or have it worked out by a third party, and once I'd explained my thinking and put other tailor-made metrics in place, it turns out that my refusal never cost me a client.

The Barcelona Principles

The PR measurement and evaluation community came together in Barcelona in June 2010 for the AMEC Second European Summit. AMEC is the

Association for Measurement and Evaluation of Communication, and it played host to organizations such as the IPR, the PRSA, the ICCO, the CIPR and the PR Global Alliance. I was there, representing the CIPR.

The 7 principles are:

1. Goal setting and measurement are important
2. Media measurement requires quantity and quality
3. AVEs are not the value of public relations
4. Social media can and should be measured
5. Measuring outcomes is preferred to measuring media results (outputs)
6. Organizational results and outcomes should be measured whenever possible
7. Transparency and replicability are paramount to sound measurement.

These principles have been criticized by some as being too simple, too basic, but that, I think, is their value. Absent consensus on the basics, the foundations, and building anything grander becomes a dicey endeavour. With these principles tucked under its belt, AMEC has already moved on to the next stage: its US Agency Research Leaders Group, chaired by Ketchum's David Rockland, is now set on attacking two questions:

- What are the 'validated metrics' to replace AVEs?
- How do you get started in measuring social media, and what are the definitions of relevant metrics?

You will know that I was particularly pleased with principle number 3. Indeed, I see that Paul Holmes of the eponymous Holmes Report was also delighted, making the astute observation that AVEs don't measure the value of advertising either, just its cost.[60] I'd never thought of it like that but it's so true and reminds PRs that advertisers have similar measurement woes. And to repeat the observations made on my blog at the time, even if best practice doesn't turn out to be as simple or even as generic as AVE (and it doesn't), we will at last have something of true value and practical insight to bring to the board table rather than a specious sum based on false assumptions using an unfounded multiplier, only addressing a fraction of the PR domain.

I'm hoping that this book contributes to the AMEC Group's deliberations, as will, I'm sure, Katie Delahaye Paine's new book *Measure What Matters.*[61] Katie is writing her book at the same time as I am writing this one, and we have shared perspectives to see how the books might relate. On that basis alone, I have no doubt that *Measure What Matters* forms a perfect complement to mine, as I'll expand upon later.

Table 5.1 sums up my stance towards tactical measurement across marketing and PR disciplines, and we'll get to the strategic level later. We will now take a look at the influencer-centric and influence-centric approaches referenced in the table.

Table 5.1: Maturity of influence approach

Maturity	Characteristics	
High	Trace the influence (the action) back to source.	Focused on business outcomes, as we should be.	Influence-centric
Medium	It's quality not quantity. Not how many people you interact with, but how and in what context?	Best practice, intelligent and you could say scientific and professional marketing and PR, and associated activities.	Influence-centric
Low	Number of followers, friends, subscribers, circulation. Empirically supported network science.	Akin to column inches and AVE – measurement because you can, not because you should.	Influencer-centric
Pitiful	Obfuscating compound measures of non-contextual trivial variables (see below). No empirical evidence.		Influencer-centric

Influencer-centric

Pitiful is a deliberately pejorative description. The pitiful and low levels of maturity described in Table 5.1 are described as influencer-centric as opposed to the influence-centricity of the higher levels. They obsess with identifying influencers on the basis that some publicly available quantities about them betray the influence they actually have on others; i.e. changing what others think or what others do. Yet, as mentioned earlier, an individual's popularity is not synonymous with the influence he or she may exert on others.

Someone's influence is not . . .

- the number of friends or followers or subscribers
- a sum of Diggs or Reddits or Stumbles or @'s or Retweets
- their website's Google's PageRank or SEOmoz's mozRank
- the number of blogs and columns they write
- the books and papers they author
- the job they have

. . . when these things are considered in isolation or out of context.

And influence is definitely not some quantity invented by a PR firm, analytics provider, or measurement and evaluation company that rolls up a number of indices and measures into some relatively arbitrary compound formula that makes any appreciation of the underlying approach, variables and mathematics completely opaque to the end-user, thereby radically attenuating any little use it may have been but in such a way that it can be nicely branded and sold as 'unique'. (Phew, I'm glad to get that off my chest.)

Since criticizing services such as Klout for doing just this sort of thing in my presentation to Monitoring Social Media Bootcamp 2010, the Klout team has expanded on its approach and ambition. The summary version is[62]:

> The Klout Score is the measurement of your overall online influence. The scores range from 0 to 100 with higher scores representing a wider and stronger sphere of influence. Klout uses over 25 variables to measure True Reach, Amplification Probability, and Network Score. The size of the sphere is calculated by measuring True Reach (engaged followers and friends vs spam bots, dead accounts, etc.). Amplification Probability is the likelihood that messages will generate retweets or spark a conversation. If the user's engaged followers are highly influential, they'll have a high Network Score.

Klout proceeds to provide a fairly diligent description. Unfortunately, it stops short of the mathematics, probably as much for intellectual property reasons as for the likelihood that most people using the service don't have the hunger to know. Today, marketing and PR professionals aren't expected to be numerate or meticulous in this sort of way, but when we discuss the emergence of the influence professional later, I associate the title with just this kind of aptitude.

A similar service, Social Mention, isn't so forthcoming as it seems to treat potential customers condescendingly. Incredulously, in answer to the question 'How does it work?' in its FAQs, it simply replies: 'It works just fine, thank you for asking.' Perhaps I'm confusing comedy for arrogance, but regardless, which professional could seriously list this service as a tool of his trade?

No standard for influence

Klout is in the business of network science, where, at the time of writing, network science is defined on Wikipedia[63] as 'a new and emerging scientific discipline that examines the interconnections among diverse physical or engineered networks, information networks, biological networks, cognitive and semantic networks, and social networks', and in a publication from the National Research Council[64] as consisting of 'the study of network representations of physical, biological, and social phenomena leading to predictive models of these phenomena.'

This is interesting and probably important work, and for that Klout should be congratulated. Nevertheless, I still have some problems with Klout, although I've tempered my language since March 2010. Klout encourages users to take its analysis of the past performance by an individual on Twitter and Facebook as an indication of future performance. It discloses that it only takes Twitter and Facebook statistics into account, but then claims in its strapline to be 'the Standard for Influence'. What about blogs and forums and product reviews, and just about any other non-Twitter contribution to the social Web? What about face-to-face, telephone, email, SMS and instant messaging? According to the Institute of Practitioners in Advertising's 2010 TouchPoints survey,[65] emailing remains the number one online activity, accounting for 20% of time online; followed by work-related Internet use at 16% and social networking at 11%, of which Twitter will only represent a fraction.

Most critically, services like Klout can only be very lightweight when it comes to monitoring the effects of influence. You've been influenced when you think in a way you wouldn't otherwise have thought, or do something you wouldn't have otherwise done, and yet the only actions Klout can detect are retweets, decisions to follow someone or add them to a list, tweet rate, and so on. This is ideal if one of your organizational objectives is to maximize retweets, etc., but I cannot imagine that 'maximize retweets, etc.' features as a stated objective in your annual report.

Where might Klout-like services stand if individuals' active and daily use of Twitter and Facebook becomes as ubiquitous as organizations' active and daily use of websites? After all, Google's PageRank algorithm is based on network science, focused on hyperlinks on webpages to other webpages, and is renowned for translating these 'votes' for webpages into search results that are relevant more often than not. The problem with this comparison is that the content is the end of the journey for Web search (at least it is today). Does the content answer the question? Does the website have the information or resources or service you were looking for? If Google thought it did yesterday, it's because others thought it did yesterday, and it probably still does today.

But in the world of personal influence – in the domain of influencer-centric measurement and analysis – we can only ever rely on proxies for personal influence that may or may not be a reliable indicator of influence and, equally importantly, we never know in which cases they might be more or less reliable. Unlike influence-centric measurement and evaluation, as we'll discuss shortly, we can never close the loop.

Interestingly, *Business Week* reported in August 2008[66] that Google has 'patent pending technology for ranking the most influential people on social networking sites', but other than a further article at Search Engine People[67] I can find nothing more recent. It might be quite similar to the approach adopted by a company called PostRank,[68] (a name noticeably similar to Google's PageRank) that's attempting to build a measure of online influence that extends beyond Twitter. From its website:

> PostRank provides the best measurement of influence for people who produce content online. PostRank tracks the engagement that each

> article generates – tweets, diggs, and comments for example – in real-time, and delivers comprehensive metrics about the content and the conversations around it. PR professionals and brands can dynamically measure the real impact that targeted influencers are having with the audience.

PostRank is doing some really interesting stuff, but of course it is only assessing a lesser facet of influence, one that's manifest in actions/outputs such as sharing, liking something, giving it the thumbs up or down, stars out of five, and commenting. It cannot pick up influence that's manifest in outcomes or in behavioural change corresponding to an organization's objectives – such as being persuaded to change political party allegiance or changing from buying brand X to brand Y.

And what if the whole premise is wrong, or even just partially wrong? What if John 'the Mow' Doe appears to be the expert on lawnmowers? What if those interested in lawnmowing retweet him and comment on his blog? But what if his views don't actually affect people's choice of Flymo over Lawn-Boy, or Bosch over Honda? What if he's an expert but not influential? We've already highlighted the pitfall of confusing popularity for influence; might we also confuse *expertise* for influence?

The complexity of influence

Stephen Waddington, Managing Director of Speed Communications, gave his thoughts on integrated marketing communications earlier. But I'm now going to quote his daughters, Ellie (11) and Freya (10), who helped their Dad to post to his blog when they and other children of the Speed staff came into the office for the day.[69]

Ellie says: 'What influences me the most on what to buy are usually my friends. My friends recommend things to me but I also look at what they're wearing and what they talk about.' And Freya says: 'I think the thing that makes me buy things is mostly my friends, they buy it then tell me about things, so I want to go and buy them.'

I'm obviously making no assertion that this sample is statistically significant – it just happens to be a nice, pertinent opener for this section.

What if we were hoping that this whole influence thing would be simple, but actually turned out to be pretty complicated? As the answer to this question lies at the heart of the matter here, let's proceed now to review the landscape through the eyes of the practitioner – the marketing agency, market researchers, the user-experience researcher and academe, including a doctor of mechanics.

The practitioner

It appears that Ellie and Freya are not atypical in regarding their friends as the leading influences in their lives. In his presentation at TEDx PennQuarter 2010, David Armano, SVP Edelman Digital, discussed various aspects of social media, including a short observation about influence from his study of a particular social media campaign.[70] Armano credited the role played by some individuals with large influence circles, assessed by variables such as number of social media friends, followers and retweets, but also recognized that 'a lot of people with smaller circles of influence also made a big difference'. He finishes his report to the audience by saying that there were different levels of influence that all needed to work together.

The marketing agency

Armano wasn't presenting any kind of quantitative conclusion, but what if small circles make more of a difference than bigger ones? This possibility seems to be supported in findings by marketing agency Razorfish in its report *Fluent: The Razorfish Social Influence Marketing Report*, 2009.[71]
  The Razorfish team studied three categories of influencer:

- *Key influencers* – have an outsized influence in specific fields on brand affinity and purchasing decisions on social platforms; typically have their own blogs, huge Twitter followings and rarely know their audiences personally.
- *Social influencers* – everyday people, typically in your consumer's social network, influencing brand affinity and purchasing decisions through consumer reviews, by updating their own status and Twitter feeds and

commenting on blogs and forums; the consumer may know the social influencers personally.

- *Known peer influencers* – typically family members or part of the consumer's inner circle; closest to both the consumer and the purchasing decision; they influence the purchasing decision most directly and have to live with the results.

In ascertaining the role each of these influencer categories plays as consumers move through the so-called marketing funnel, the report finds:

> Known peer influence tops the list, but social media – including corporate and independent blogs produced by key influencers – and user-generated content (UGC) from social influencers, play an influential role that meets or beats traditional marketing efforts.
>
> When asked how certain sources influence respondents in the awareness, consideration and action phases of making a purchase, respondents consistently attribute strong to heavy influence to word-of-mouth from known peers, both online and off. This bears out across all phases, with influence nearly doubling during the awareness and action phases, as compared to the consideration phase.

Table 5.2 shows the diagram from the report portraying the exact figures.

Market researchers

Invoke Solutions, Harris Interactive and Forrester Research have all studied this issue.

Invoke Solutions

The market research firm Invoke Solutions reached the following conclusions following a 300-person study of active social media users[72]:

> Generally, participants trusted information most when it was generated by friends, or people they know regardless of content form.

Table 5.2: The role of influencers in the marketing funnel, Razorfish, Fluent report, 2009, reproduced with permission

No influence % (1&2)	Awareness Phase Neutral (3)	Heavy influence % (4&5)
5	**Close family and friends**	78
17	Independent bloggers	59
22	Contribute to YouTube, etc.	49
20	Corporate bloggers	46
22	Anonymous peer reviews	34

No influence % (1&2)	Consideration Phase Neutral (3)	Heavy influence % (4&5)
23	Contribute to YouTube, etc.	49
19	Anonymous peer reviews	43
6	**Close family and friends**	42
35	Independent bloggers	23
47	Corporate bloggers	20

No influence % (1&2)	Action Phase Neutral (3)	Heavy influence % (4&5)
5	**Close family and friends**	79
22	Anonymous peer reviews	43
38	Independent bloggers	21
51	Contribute to YouTube, etc.	18
50	Corporate bloggers	17

Known Peer Influencers = Close family and friends
Social Influencers = Contributors to YouTube, Flickr, etc., and anonymous peer reviews
Key Influencers = Independent bloggers and corporate bloggers
Percentages do not add up to 100 because neutral respondents are not reported here

> However Facebook posts by companies were either 'trusted completely' or 'trusted somewhat' by 41% of respondents and company blog posts fared nearly as well at 36%.
>
> The most important factors in trusting a social media content source were the open nature of dialog, and the quality of comments and content.

> Somewhat surprisingly, few participants rated length of participation (15%) and number of fellow fans, followers and participants (12%) as extremely important.

Harris Interactive

The pollster Harris Interactive undertook some research in 2010, *Speak Now or Forever Hold Your Tweets.*[73] On asking those surveyed what influenced their decision 'a great deal' to use or not use a particular company, brand or product:

- 71% said reviews from family members or friends;
- 46% said reviews in newspapers or magazine articles;
- 45% said reviews from friends or people they follow on social networking websites;
- 33% said reviews on blogs and message boards;
- 10% said reviews by celebrities.

Forrester Research

In Forrester Research's April 2010 report *Peer Influence Analysis* by Augie Ray and Josh Bernoff, the executive summary (reproduced with permission) begins:

> For marketers seeking the sort of reach offered by advertising, social media has posed a challenge. Based on our surveys, we now know that people in the US generate more than 500 billion online impressions on each other regarding products and services – more than one-fourth the number of impressions advertisers make. Furthermore, 16% of the online consumers generate 80% of these impressions.

The report authors describe an analysis technique they call Peer Influence Analysis designed to determine how many impressions social applications create, who has the greatest influence (online) and how influence differs between product or service categories. Based on surveying 10,000 consumers about their online social participation, 'influence impressions' are calculated by the number of tweets and updates people make and the number of friends or followers who may read them. There's commonality here with traditional measures of advertising reach, a comparison drawn in the executive summary, and the influence impressions analysis stops short of looking for engagement as emphasized by such as Katie Delahaye Paine, Econsultancy and PostRank.

The analysis also looks at 'influence posts', defined as ratings, reviews, forum posts, blog posts and comments, and the report points out that it's impossible to measure accurately the number of people who potentially read each influence post.

The report identifies two types of what it calls Mass Influencers. In homage to Malcolm Gladwell's book of 2000, *The Tipping Point*,[74] there are Mass Connectors (11 million people responsible for 80% of impressions) and Mass Mavens (24 million people responsible for 80% of the influence posts). Some people belong to both groups, making a total of 29 million Mass Influencers (all numbers relate to the USA).

The report states:

> You do not and cannot know the identity of the vast majority of your Mass Influencers. . . . You can't engage them individually the way you would a small handful of Social Broadcasters – the influential bloggers or Twitterers you can reach with social PR. Instead, you must reach out to them efficiently, with mass social media marketing techniques.

It appears that Ray and Bernoff are in two minds about *The Tipping Point*. On one hand they pay respect to its lead characters, and on the other hand they conclude that things are nowhere near as polarized or as simple as *The Tipping Point* asserts.

(One last point on this report: Why would any social media marketer be 'seeking the sort of reach offered by advertising', as written in the first sentence of the executive summary? I'd much rather *not* pay to reach those I cannot influence, or those I don't wish to influence me. The last I knew, I wasn't in the market for eyeliner, double-glazing or a skiing holiday, yet someone has paid to 'reach' me on each of these in the last 24 hours. For clarity, this is different to our earlier recognition of the new stakeholder role of 'netizen'. Their role demands that we relate to their use of information technologies once they have declared themselves to be netizens in our domain.)

User experience researcher

Paul Adams is a senior user experience researcher at Google. I'm looking forward to reading his book, *Social Circles,*[75] which at the time of writing is scheduled to hit book shelves July 2011. Paul shares some of his findings ahead of the book's release in a presentation *Bridging the gap between our online and offline social network,*[76] and some quotes from that presentation about his research findings are pertinent to our topic:

> The role of 'influentials' is overestimated.
>
> Understanding how people influence each other is not simple. It's certainly not as simple as many people believe – that there are a small number of very influential people in society, and if you reach and influence them, they will influence hundreds, thousands and even millions of others. This is the basis for 'The Law of the Few' as described in *The Tipping Point*, and many business people subscribe to this theory. After *The Tipping Point* became a bestseller, many researchers studied whether or not it is real. Some studies concluded that there are in fact people in society who have great influence over others. But most research studies concluded that other factors play a much bigger part in how people are influenced.
>
> Whether someone can be influenced is as important as the strength of the influencer.
>
> We're most influenced by the people around us.

Academe

In *Determining Influential Users in Internet Social Networks* in the *Journal of Marketing Research,*[77] August 2010, Drs Trusov, Bodapati and Bucklin find that not all 'friends' are created equal:

> Firms operating SN [social networking] sites observe an 'overt' network of friends, defined according to who added whom as a friend. Most of the links in this network are 'weak' in the sense that the relationships

> do not significantly affect behaviour in the network. It is of interest to identify the 'strong' links (i.e., the links corresponding to friends who affect the user's behaviour).

They also find that:

> relatively few so-called friends are actually significant influencers of a given user's behaviour (22% is the sample mean), while substantial heterogeneity across users also exists. The authors also find that descriptors from user profiles . . . lack the power to determine who, per se, is influential.
>
> . . . friend counts and profile views also fall short of being able to identify influential site members, especially for the most important 5–10% of users.

Dr Duncan Watts isn't beloved of marketers. He's applied his physics degree and doctorate in theoretical and applied mechanics to the study of information contagion. In perhaps the best summary of his work to date – a Fast Company article from February 2008, *Is the Tipping Point Toast?*[78] – he is quoted as saying: 'Influentials don't govern person-to-person communication. We all do.' He isn't beloved apparently because this is interpreted to be bad news for marketers.

The article continues:

> Watts believes this is because a trend's success depends not on the person who starts it, but on how susceptible the society is overall to the trend – not how persuasive the early adopter is, but whether everyone else is easily persuaded.
>
> . . . 'If society is ready to embrace a trend, almost anyone can start one – and if it isn't, then almost no one can', Watts concludes. To succeed with a new product, it's less a matter of finding the perfect hipster to infect and more a matter of gauging the public's mood. Sure, there'll always be a first mover in a trend. But since she generally stumbles into that role by chance, she is, in Watts's terminology, an 'accidental Influential'.

The article capitalizes Influential in deference to Jon Berry's and Ed Keller's 2003 book *The Influentials*,[79] a book with theories *Publishers Weekly* described as 'compelling and exceedingly well researched, and should be a boon to anyone looking to promote the next big thing'. Dr Watts counters the ideas presented by Berry and Keller – and Gladwell:

> No researcher, he points out – including Keller – ever analyses interactions between specific Influentials and the friends they're supposedly influencing; no one observes influence in action. In essence, Keller appeals to common sense – our intuitive sense of how the world works. Watts thinks common sense is misleading.

Innovation-driven complexity

Innovations are empowering each and every individual stakeholder, and each and every employee of organizational stakeholders, to set their news / information / content schedule. It's what they want, when they want it, and how they want it.

Web users have had the ability for several years to customize a homepage, subscribe to RSS feeds, and record media they want to watch later, but for me the advent in 2010 of personalized social news streams[80] marked the beginning of everyone having their own sophisticated customized channel. Such channels are tailored uniquely and automatically from our own subscriptions, our friends' subscriptions and recommendations, and automated 'if you like that, you'll like this' discovery. In my presentation at Internet World 2005, London, I labelled precisely this eventuality myChannel.

Two billion Internet users. Two billion channels.

The ramifications of myChannel for influence professionals include:

- Considerably more fragmentation of the target audience of communications campaigns.
- Less precise timing of delivery.
- Less certainty of how each recipient is receiving the information.
- Increased opportunity to provide niche information.

- Greater opportunity for innovation in inviting and securing interaction.
- The need for new mechanisms for gauging communication success.

Why do we think it's not complex?

Let's take a look at how this reality manifests itself in the day of a PR consultant: one that's living the dream in 1991, and one that's teetering on the edge in 2011. Complexity doesn't feature in 1991; everything is quite manageable, thank you. By 2011, however, things have become quite complicated indeed. A similar comparison could be drawn for an advertising executive, of course.

We're in 1991 and your campaign execution demands a vanilla media relations outreach. You need to contact 20 journalists across your target publications and broadcast media – your tier 1. You might also want to 'spray' the rest with a wire distribution. Effectively then, you have 21 points of focus. A few of the target journalists are freelance and write for two or three key publications, and as you expect a bit of syndication, you have approximately three-dozen media to track.

The campaign results in potential coverage across this media, requiring assessment of sentiment (positive / neutral / negative) and readership. A clippings service sweeps up the tertiary coverage for you, which you will treat as tier 2 and weight accordingly. A share of voice analysis reviews all coverage in your 30-odd tier 1 media, and teases out the mentions of your brand, your product, and those of your nearest competitors.

This is simple stuff. There are no mathematical products here, just some simple high school arithmetic based on averages and spreads.

Now let's go back to the future, to 2011. As we've seen, communication and media technologies proliferate and company-to-customer communication now competes for attention with customer-to-customer communication. Active and passive customer-to-customer and customer-to-company communication is multi-channelled and in the public domain. The format of communication has expanded massively beyond the press release to include blog posts, podcasts, video, Twitter, games, live Web chats, etc.

This means that you now have many different ways and channels to engage with customers and prospects, and they have many ways to engage with you and each other. You employ continuous, active listening, and you're effectively involved in thousands – possibly millions – of relationships.

Where should I listen and how should I make sense of it, and what demands a response and what should I say and when should I say it, and to whom should I say it and where should I say it, and in which format should I say it? When you multiply these possibilities together it becomes immediately clear that you're trying to deal with massive complexity, at least relative to your colleague from 1991. We have many more permutations and complexity than any human can juggle independently in a meaningful way.

Following our roundup of some of the research into the sources of influence, and this quick 'a day in the life of' comparison, we have to ask why many marketers and PR professionals appear to be so fixated on identifying 'the few' – the individuals who supposedly have the rest of the world in their hands. In trying to explain the differences between the evidence and practice, I find myself thinking about two contributory factors.

The first factor is one that Paul Adams also refers to: an apparent widespread faith in some of the assertions made by Malcolm Gladwell in *The Tipping Point*. It appears to have almost single-handedly influenced marketers' regard for the power of 'the few'; how ironic that one man can exert such influence! Other works, such as *The Influentials*, compounded the consensus.

I believe the other contributory factor is a self-narrowing of focus. While I have nothing but anecdotal evidence for this personally, I get the feeling that some marketing and PR practitioners are quite simply in denial; they don't believe that things could have become quite so complicated. They want to believe in *The Tipping Point* and *The Influentials*. They appear, on the whole, to be far more comfortable approaching a communications campaign in a world nearer to one extreme – in which, for example, a TV superstar espouses her choice of product and everyone else obligingly falls in line (think of Oprah's book club), than to the other extreme, in which an individual is more influenced by the 150 associates nearest to them than by the other six or so billion combined. Think about the movies you've seen, or music you've bought after recommendations from friends. And I chose 150 because that figure is usually referred to as the Dunbar number – the number of relationships each of us can typically maintain, which itself features in *The Tipping Point* of course.

I hope this is accepted as a plain observation, rather than any kind of haughty criticism. The Fast Company article, however, reports a perspective that's a little more charged:

> Joe Pilotta, research VP for a firm called Big Research (and one of Watts's bigger fans), suspects marketers cling to their belief in Influentials partly because they're lazy. 'They love the idea of needing to reach only a small group of people to 'tip' a product,' he says with a laugh. Plus, it strokes their egos.
>
> 'Think about it. You're saying, 'I am in control – I am the biggest influencer, because I am going to influence the influencers!' It's an arrogance that only the corporate world could enjoy'.

Given that the idea of 'the few' has such traction, and obviously examples plainly exist, you will notice I have invested most of my time here providing the counter balance. For my part, it's obvious that there's an Oprah (and Watts would argue that if you could re-run history there would likely be someone like Oprah, just not Oprah). Also, things often appear to come 'out of nowhere'. It's complex. And to clarify that observation, complex systems can sometimes demonstrate behaviours that appear simple and deterministic, and sometimes they appear non-linear, random, chaotic.[81] It's definitely an area worthy of more analysis and potential commercialization, so do get in touch if you'd like to support this work; I even registered the domain name brandcomplexity. com a few years back in anticipation.

Influence-centric

I define an influence-centric approach as consisting of two complementary foci. On one hand we focus relentless attention on those who have already been influenced in the way we wanted: for example, they have already bought our product, voted for our party, stopped their anti-social behaviour. I refer to this simply as the focus on the influenced. On the other hand, albeit closely related, we dedicate ourselves to finding out how influence has recently been achieved: for example, why has someone just bought our product, or our competitor's? This is tracing influence.

If this sounds like nothing new to you, you're right; although information technologies may help us to do both more effectively and efficiently and we're lending it fresh emphasis and integrating it into a new framework.

Focus on the influenced

Modern organizations have sloughed off the idea that as soon as a new customer has handed over the cash or signed the contract they can be completely ignored as the effort continues to be focused solely on the latest prospects. The concept of customer lifetime value is well and truly entrenched nowadays, and modern organizations apportion some effort to delivering post-sales service and maintaining customer loyalty to the benefit of both.

Nevertheless, as a consumer of products and services myself, from for-profits and not for-profits, and as a business man, I know some kind of cost-optimization is at play; in other words, what's the minimal investment we have to make to get 'enough' customers back for more? Organizations can cope with the typical customer paths, but too often you get the feeling that post-sales customer service processes can't always cope adequately with the inevitable deviations from that path.

Here's a tale of how not to focus on the influenced. Everyone has stories like this, so I won't bore you with intricacies but leave you with the overall flavour.

I needed a new mobile phone and picked a model that I had played with earlier in the year at Mobile World Congress and selected a retailer based on price. The phone didn't do something I was told it would do by the manufacturer at the Congress, by shop staff on two separate occasions prior to buying the phone, and by customer support after the purchase. Nevertheless, both the manufacturer and retailer refused to help me in any way and I ended up having to sell the phone to someone for whom the absence of the capability in question was not a problem.

But, I was asked if I would like to join the manufacturer's online community. I was told that there were lots of reasons why I should (although the only aspect I was interested in wasn't referenced at all). And the retailer entreated me to earn £50 for each new customer I brought them, would you believe it. How dare they not marry my negative experience to their decisions to make these invitations? And the only reason I don't go so far as to name and shame both the manufacturer and the retailer – to share the unlove I feel – is because my editor would strike the names out later anyway. But rest assured, I don't waste opportunities in other situations.

And here's a similarly personal tale of how to focus on the influenced.

Many of the geeky types I hang out with began to get Apple MacBooks. On talking with them and experiencing the machines for myself, I fell in love with the engineering if not the price tag; seriously, twice the price of equivalently powered PC notebooks. But the recommendations were strong enough to get me to take the plunge. It hasn't been a flawless product experience but the relationship I feel Apple has forged with me is. I can meet with 'Geniuses' (Apple's name for its support staff) at my local Apple store's Genius Bar and they actually help me and things get fixed. I ran a customer service training course for a client a while back during which the CEO claimed a 'Genius' had invested six hours fixing his machine.

I also trust Apple to tell me where it stands. I'll buy its MacBooks and iMacs, but because Apple is explicit about its closed approach with iPhone and iPad, I know to avoid them (I'm a champion of open approaches).

I refer to this policy as investment rather than cost for good reason. Not only is Apple sufficiently confident in its abilities to price some of this post-sales support into its purchase price, but they also know that future revenue growth lies in this direction. That CEO and I are walking, talking, unpaid salespeople for Apple MacBooks. Apple focused on the influenced to their benefit and ours.

Of course, for those readers familiar with the Net Promoter Score, these stories will remind you of Fred Reichheld's so-called ultimate question: 'Would you feel comfortable recommending us to others?'[82] Reichheld asserts that this question, demanding as it does a response from a customer on an 11-point ordinal scale and resulting in a Net Promoter Score, belies the future revenue growth prospects of any organization as well as any other customer loyalty test but does so more practicably and in a manner an organization's employees can more easily relate to.

Reichheld claims that the best way to create loyalty is to "show your partners that loyalty is a logical strategy for the pursuit of self-interest when self-interest is defined in the context of lifelong success", where his use of "partners" refers to all stakeholders, including customers and employees.

Focus on the influenced is outcome oriented (e.g. promoter score and revenue growth, securing insights into and understanding of current customers and other stakeholders) rather than output oriented (e.g. column inches, 'opportunities to see', feedback forms completed).

One of the phrases from my ebook that I repeat most often is: The discontented spread their discontent. The neutral say nothing. The contented say nothing. The delighted spread their delight.

Why would any world-class organization be happy with any level of discontent when discontent may be worse than not having won the business in the first place? When discontent is the number one enemy of achieving organizational goals? And when delighted customers are one of the most powerful engines of organizational success, why wouldn't any world-class organization not pursue relationships with its customers to a service level that moves them up through neutral and contented to delight?

Conversation and customer service is PR and marketing.

Note how 'the influenced' means those who have done something they otherwise wouldn't have done (e.g. buy your product) and is not a contraction of 'the positively influenced', i.e. those who have come round to our point of view, as it might be in more casual parlance. Focus on the influenced is not then the same as focus on fans. A fan is already delighted and because fans spread that delight they are already known for being delighted, whereas the influenced have simply become customers (or other type of stakeholder) and can be discontent, neutral, content or delighted.

This distinction is important in the light of Jim Novo's review of *Firm-Created Word-of-Mouth Communication: Evidence from a Field Test* by Godes, David, Mayzlin, and Dina, published in *Marketing Science*, 2009.[83] This field test aimed to identify the conditions for effectiveness in a word-of-mouth campaign and came to two related conclusions:

- Investing in encouraging word of mouth by less loyal (defined as not highly loyal) customers and acquaintances (not necessarily friends) was found to be more effective than working with highly loyal customers whose evangelism and continued custom didn't need the investment.

- Highly loyal customers are not as effective in spreading word of mouth to drive incremental sales because this is their normal mode; their network already appreciates their advocacy.

Note the emphasis on incremental sales. This research was not designed to test any hypotheses relating to the criticality of ongoing advocacy by the highly loyal (the delighted in our framework here) to the maintenance of current sales, but it does raise some interesting questions.

Given that delighted customers are already delighted, what advantage might there be in prioritizing resources towards delighting the other customers who don't yet feel it? Or is that the quickest route to tarnishing the elation felt by the delighted to the point at which they become less so?

How might an emphasis on the potential of an individual to become an evangelist, or on their potential to bring new business through the door – that is, an emphasis that rides over their personal lifetime value – redefine CRM customer stratification strategies? And do the delighted only spread their delight to others of similar sales potential?

In their 2004 book *Strategy Maps: Converting Intangible Assets into Tangible Outcomes*,[84] Kaplan and Norton make the point:

> Customers who act as apostles or owners can provide far more lifetime value than a large number of merely loyal customers who maintain or even expand their purchasing behaviour but do not recruit new customers or provide ideas for product and service improvements.

Vanessa DiMauro, CEO and Strategy Consultant, Leader Networks, pointed me to a statement reportedly made by Netflix in a 2003 conference call. In response to a challenge that Netflix was discriminating its service delivery to heavy and supposedly unprofitable customers, the reported response came back[85]:

> Since marketing is one of our largest costs, we tend to look at those heavy users actually quite positively. We may not be getting as much

gross profit on them but they tend to be heavily evangelizing the service to their friends.

But best laid plans and all that – Vanessa also pointed me to a number of threads demonstrating perhaps that those heavier users weren't quite feeling the love,[86] including this comment from an evangelizer bemoaning the unannounced loss of a treasured feature:

Adam M. said:

This is a sad development. I hope this is not a sign of continual non-fan friendly decisions. Don't you guys realize that the supposed less than 2% of people who are using the friends tab are probably your biggest advocates? Of my 26 friends, I have personally got 1/3 of them to sign up for Netflix. Maybe I'll have to convince them to start using RedBoxes.

Redbox, of course, is a competitor. There's not much more I can add to Adam M.'s declaration except that focus on the influenced is a good place to start tracing influence too.

Tracing influence

Tracing influence is all about seeking to close that loop we said influencer-centric approaches couldn't do.

Why did you buy that particular TV, that particular holiday, those particular shoes? Why did you read that particular book and rent that particular film? Why do you support that particular football team? Why do you give to that particular charity? Why did you choose that particular bank? Why do you get your coffee there in particular? Why that particular religion? Why that particular destination for your next vacation?

We're all human, so what better Petri dish to start with than one's own choices? How, where, when and why have you been influenced? And who and what contributed to the influence?

We've already seen that this isn't a new area of study, and I'm sure your self-reflecting findings won't be any different to the research conclusions. It's complex. Or in words that mean much the same, it depends on very many things, some expected and some unexpected, that may combine in expected or unexpected ways.

Some choices are influenced by one or two over-riding influences. Some support the Red Sox because they grew up in Boston. I'm going to Sydney for my vacation because that's where my friends live. Some choices are an incredible amalgam of influences from various sources at various times and of various impact. For example, the choice of airline I'll fly. It's a mix of opinions and impressions that get tangled over time and impinge on your choices in conscious and unconscious ways.

If we can't always unpick our own processing of influences, no one else is going to do it unless it's a psychologist with a couch and a few months to spare. But that shouldn't deter us from having a go as long as we assign to the results a suitable statistical significance. And if we can get so carried away with something like Klout, which works on an incredibly narrow influencer-centric dataset with all the flaws we listed earlier, surely we can become even more excited working with an equally narrow influence-centric dataset.

Chaos

You may be asking how I can reconcile tracing influence with my earlier reference to chaos. Well, systems that exhibit chaotic behaviour, unpredictability, at some times may also be predictable with certain assigned probabilities at other times. We need not look any further than the weather system for an example. On occasions the weather can be predicted with high accuracy. In some parts of the world, and for some parts of the year, tomorrow and the day after will have weather just like today. And, equally, we've all left the house without an umbrella on 'good' advice, only to be drenched.

Despite the chaos, weather forecasting is economically important. Traders buy and sell commodity crop futures and insurers base the price of crop yield insurance on long-term forecasts, for example – and, of course, it is also socially important information. To picnic or not to picnic?

The same applies to tracing influence. Just because it's difficult, and because it turns out to be more accurate some times and entirely unpredictable at other times, doesn't mean that it does not have significant value. And if we recall the Fast Company article reporting Watts as pointing out that no one ever analyses interactions or observes influence in action, that's exactly what I'm proposing. More ambitiously, I'm not just talking about doing so in an academic context; I'm proposing that influence professionals should do so operationally.

Influence traceability

Obviously I'm not advocating something too simple like last-click or last-touch attribution. Last-touch describes the association of the value of a sale (a 'conversion' in Web analytics terminology) to the link the customer last clicked or the content they last viewed, and is widely understood now to be an oversimplification that could lead to sub-optimal or downright poor decision making. Arguably, the touches that precede the last-touch are more important most of the time.

Table 5.3 portrays what I call the influence traceability quadrant. While its name doesn't exactly trip off the tongue, it helps us to focus our attention and at the same time keep mindful of the stuff we're ignoring.

I won't expand yet on what I refer to in the quadrants as digital detritus; we'll come to that later. We'll also see how the knowledge we ascertain from the 'self-unaware digitally accessible' quadrant might facilitate self-learning, thereby promoting the flow in question to the 'aware digitally accessible' quadrant.

Table 5.3: The influence traceability quadrants

Self-aware	Elicitation, marketing research	Opt-in sharing of digital detritus / logs, existing tracking systems, elicitation, marketing research
Self-unaware	Inaccessible (or at least not economically accessible)	Opt-in sharing of digital detritus / logs, existing tracking systems
	Digitally inaccessible	**Digitally accessible**
	For example, broadcast, outdoor and in-store advertising and promotion	For example, email and IM with friend, forum participation, visited pertinent webpage (stored in browser history), SMS history

We could also divide the digitally accessible column in two: digitally accessible now, and potentially digitally accessible in the future subject to the technological development of products and services and the customer's decision to adopt these products and share the data with you. Again, more on that later.

For now, let's review where marketing research fits in here.

Marketing research

I presented some differences between traditional market research and continuous engagement at the Insight 2006 Market Research show in London. Figure 5.1 portrays the ad hoc or periodic market research based on the well-established sequence of define, plan, commission, gather, analyse, interpret and learn. Figure 5.2 is one way to show continuous engagement with some fraction of one's customers and prospects.

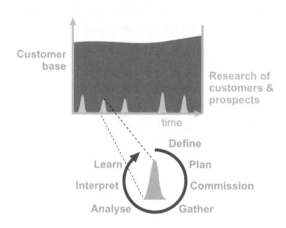

Figure 5.1: Traditional market research

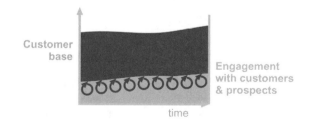

Figure 5.2: Continuous engagement

Table 5.4: Comparing market research and continuous engagement

Market research	Continuous engagement
Ad hoc or regular intervals	Continuous
One-way (and often needs the carrot of a prize, gift or payment)	Two-way (mutually rewarding)
Unemotional	Emotional
Independent of loyalty	Inculcates brand loyalty
Tight focus	Wide focus
Sequential parameters	Multi-parametric
Designed to achieve statistical confidence	Emphasis on detecting weak signals

With their emphasis on learning about customers' and prospects' needs and desires to inform management decision making, we're talking here about the 3rd influence flow (our stakeholders' influence with us). Of course, the influence flowing into us might consist of the insights uncovered on employing market research and continuous engagement to learning about all the other flows.

Table 5.4 tabulates major differences between market research and continuous engagement. Traditional market research is ad hoc or periodic. This could mean your last dataset is getting on a bit. It could lead you to trying to read between the lines because the last survey didn't ask exactly the question you now need answering. Your market may be speeding up faster than your research frequency. You will probably need to ask new questions, but want to continue trending previous survey data.

Traditional market research has a one-way benefit – what's in it for your respondents? Have you ever wondered if they're answering your questions conscientiously? Are they likely to benefit or suffer as a consequence of the information they share with you?

Traditional market research is unemotional – so, quite simply, do respondents care? For what duration can you keep them interested? How many times can you change the subject before the respondent's brain starts to hurt?

Ad hoc, one-way, unemotional interaction does not drive brand loyalty. But of course such research was never intended to, and in fact most of these characteristics presented polemically here as disadvantages are in fact by design. Research specialists consider them as advantages.

Research is a specialism demanding numeracy and a working knowledge of research methodology and statistical technique. It's not for casual cause that Katie Delahaye Paine pointed out in an interview I recorded with her May 2010[87] that too many PR people 'run for the hills' when regression analysis is mentioned. She avows that the new PR professional must graduate with a solid foundation in statistics.

Research methodologies have accrued massive strength from two centuries of statistical knowledge. Continuous engagement via the social Web, on the other hand, is still in its infancy.

Continuous engagement does have some advantages in complement to research, not least of which is that your customers, prospects and all stakeholders discuss anything and everything on the social Web unprompted. For each topic, you can choose to interact or just listen, and you can also seed the conversation with topics that are relevant to your business tomorrow, not just today. Test their reaction and harvest value-added feedback, qualitative and quantitative. This book was never intended to be a social media how-to, so I'll leave it to other books to describe this process further (see the recommended reading list on the website).

Traditional research addresses a limited sequence of parameters, whereas you can explore multiple parameters on the social Web. Your product roadmap may encompass hundreds of parametric permutations, in which case, depending on the nature of your products and services of course, you could choose to present ideas based on 'runs' (parametric groupings based on Taguchi orthogonal arrays) to your most loyal and valued social media participants – a grander version of A/B testing if you like, where two versions of your product or service are presented to two different groups of customer to see which performs better. You've heard of user-generated-content, well this is consumer-generated-products or consumer-honed-products.

So-called 'weak signals', early but faint signs of things to come, are easily overlooked in traditional research as statistically insignificant, but your social Web analytics can be trained to help to identify tomorrow's challenge or opportunity today. If you subscribe to the conclusions presented by Surowiecki in *The Wisdom of Crowds*[88] you will feel that your chances of coming out with a well-received and successful product are improved if you incorporate feedback from the social Web into your product development roadmap.

In fact, this constant observation of the zeitgeist and proactive inclusion of social Web participants in your product development can place you weeks if not months ahead of your competition in timely new product launches; that is, until they catch up with this application of social Web analytics and get their 3rd influence flow (our stakeholders' influence with us) humming too, of course.

Call centres

Inferring knowledge from digital information in order to trace influence is worthwhile but hard work. How much easier might it be to actually speak with stakeholders directly? I've adopted a sarcastic tone more than once when I've reminded Web-obsessed companies of this amazing new technology called the telephone.

What might we deduce from the subtleties of communication via tone of voice and emotional tenor that, given very few of us are world-class novelists or poets, is lost in written form (assuming, of course, that this one-on-one exchange can be captured effectively, i.e. digitally)?

I always invite my clients to review their stance towards call centres and associated customer service touch points by insisting that they consider for a moment a call centre as being predominantly a profit centre rather than cost centre; contemplate it as part of the business that predominantly contributes to revenue and profit growth rather than cost growth. If your organization pivots on how well it practises influencing stakeholders and being influenced by them, why is a call centre non-core? Why would anyone think this could be outsourced or off-shored? Those of your team who actually speak with customers and prospects are the closest your organization gets to the real world as it exists today. These team members are an essential component of the membrane between your organization and the world in which it operates. The more permeable you make this membrane, and the more you tend to its effectiveness in ensuring that the influence flows work for you, then the more likely you'll have an organization that is heightened to identify opportunity ahead of the pack and is alert to the danger of the continued pursuit of out-dated strategies. Sure, third-party call centre operators will say they can still make this work for you, but how easily can you rotate all staff into the call centre at some point during the year? Seriously, every person in your organization should man the phones regularly, just as they should keep an eye on what's happening online.

> 'Hi, Helen here, how can I help? . . . Well, I spend most of my time here in engineering and I'm taking customer calls today to keep up to date on what customers love and hate. I don't know the answer to your question but I'm sitting next to Bob who's doing the same as me today. He looks after our stores so he might know . . . let me just grab him.'

Human. Open. Real. Authentic.

Just ask Apple, if they'd tell you, how its 'Geniuses' and retail staff are regarded internally. Why did Zappos, 'a service company that just happens to sell shoes', decide they'd 'rather spend money on things that improve the customer experience than on marketing'?[89] Why is calls-per-hour, a metric that conveys the message 'service that customer as quickly as possible and get the hell on with the next one', usually considered a more important operational metric than time spent understanding and delighting the customer?

The Six Influence Flows are a lifeblood of your organization: online, on the phone and face-to-face.

Marketing mix modelling

I consider tracing influence to be a most suitable time series data input to marketing mix modelling – the process of applying multivariate regressions and other statistical analyses to sales and marketing data to forecast the impact of future marketing efforts and thereby establish the optimum (hopefully) mix of marketing investment.

Summary

- Avoid the trap of measurement because we can, rather than because we should

- Advertising value equivalence (AVE) is not the value of public relations – it's a complete waste of time and effort
- The Barcelona Principles describe seven foundation principles of PR measurement and evaluation
- Influence-centric approaches are mature and recommended; influencer-centric approaches are considerably less mature and not recommended
- Influence-centric approaches are focused on business outcomes
- There is no standard way to determine an individual's influence
- An individual's expertise is not synonymous with that person's influence
- There are many specious measures that no self respecting professional could recommend beyond their casual interest value
- The vast majority of analysis and research concludes that we are influenced more often by friends and family than by so-called 'influentials'
- The conclusions of *The Tipping Point* are overly simplistic and probably plain wrong
- The processes of exerting influence and being influenced are complex
- Innovation is driving complexity
- Practitioners show signs of wanting to ignore this complexity, perhaps because they wouldn't then know where to start
- Influence-centricity entails focusing on the influenced and tracing influence
- Customers who proactively attract other customers to an organization or brand are incredibly valuable and are known by various names, including apostles, evangelists and owners
- Tracing influence aims to understand how influence flows and may inform marketing mix modelling
- Marketing research and continuous engagement complement each other
- Why would anyone want to outsource call centres – which are goldmines of influence information?

Now it's time to see how everything we've discussed so far fits into business performance management (BPM). In the next chapter we take our lead from the most popular BPM approach, the Balanced Scorecard.

6

Management and measurement are inseparable. Things that get measured get done, or, to change the emphasis subtly and probably more accurately, people perform as they are measured. In other words, measurement isn't some passive eye taking it all in and reporting back to the brain; it is an active, dynamic management tool as well as a feedback mechanism. It is also, from my experience in engineering, manufacturing, software, marketing and PR, one of the least well understood, neglected and, not uncommonly, misused aspects of management.

Some definitions:

- *Measurement* – the action of measuring something; ascertaining the size, amount, or degree of something by using an instrument or device; assessing the importance, effect, or value of something.
- *Evaluation* – the making of a judgement about the amount, number, or value of something.
- *Metric* – a system or standard of measurement; (in business) a set of figures or statistics that measure results.

You may have heard the phrase 'measurement and evaluation' bandied around; well it appears that 'evaluation' doesn't really add any meaning that 'measurement' doesn't convey alone. Rather than consider it redundant however, I like to think that 'evaluation' takes the qualitative role, leaving 'measurement' to focus on the quantitative aspects. Measurement and evaluation – quantitative and qualitative.

Business performance management (BPM) requires the judicious selection and application of a number of metrics. For our use of the term here, please interpret 'business' to include all variety of organizations, not just the profit-making type the word often conveys. (I would have preferred 'organization performance management' but this term is not in common use.)

Before we dive into the Influence Scorecard, let's take a tour of the leading BPM approach in use today: the Balanced Scorecard and the accompanying strategy maps. (Readers familiar with the Balanced Scorecard might wish to skim through this part.) It should, I hope, be obvious that I coined the term Influence Scorecard in homage to the Balanced Scorecard, intending to augment the latter with the former in light of the material we've covered so far and, hopefully, provide a way forward for embedding the influence processes into an organization at all levels and respond to the eternal question of return on investment.

An overview

First let me caveat this section. I aim here simply to give the briefest introduction to business performance management as encompassed by the Balanced Scorecard approach pioneered by Prof. Robert Kaplan and Dr David Norton. This introduction aims solely to be sufficient in helping me to communicate how our influence framework fits in. It cannot be in-depth, for that would take a whole book or five. Indeed, if you're serious about getting up to speed on this management approach I recommend the following books, all by Kaplan and Norton, approaching them in chronological order until you've had your fill: *The Balanced Scorecard* (1996), *The Strategy Focused Organization* (2000), *Strategy Maps* (2004), *Alignment* (2006), and *The Execution Premium* (2008), all from Harvard Business School Press.

According to the Balanced Scorecard Institute[90]:

> The Balanced Scorecard transforms an organization's strategic plan from an attractive but passive document into the 'marching orders' for the organization on a daily basis. It provides a framework that not only

provides performance measurements, but helps planners to identify what should be done and measured. It enables executives to truly execute their strategies.

It is a management system (not only a measurement system) that enables organizations to clarify their vision and strategy and translate them into action.

Business 101 – the problem

Here's the problem with business 101 as it pre-dated the Balanced Scorecard. The objective of business is to ensure that more money comes in over an acceptable timeframe than goes out and covers the cost of the capital employed to fund the business during that time. Basically, the business should make its owners more money than they might make elsewhere for the same risk, and definitely more than they'd make leaving the capital in the bank. So it's all about money – the return (profit) on investment (the capital at risk), or ROI for short.

It's also about money for non-profit organizations. They may set overarching non-financial goals, but a less efficient use of money means less effective progress towards those non-financial goals. A non-profit organization must excel at bringing in funds and employing those funds efficiently and effectively.

But how do you track financial performance, whether your objective is to maximize returns or maximize efficient and effective use of funds to meet the end goals?

Step up the triumvirate of financial reporting:

- *Profit and loss statement* – or P&L for short, reports over a specified timeframe how much money you've earned (your revenue), how much you've spent (your expenses), and the difference between the two (your profit, or loss).
- *The cash flow statement* – is a report that indicates whether the business has enough cash at a certain date to pay its current liabilities (the bills it needs to pay now and very shortly).

- *The balance sheet* – reports the overall status of your finances at a certain date; it totals all your assets and subtracts all your liabilities to compute your overall net worth.

These reports are essential to all organizations, but it's become apparent that while they are very capable of quantifying business performance historically, they're less than ideal instruments by which to orchestrate business day-to-day and week-to-week. Senior management in any business will hear phrases such as 'we aim to close last month by the 12th' and 'we're still working to close last quarter'. In other words, these reports represent the past; how we performed last month, or last quarter, or last year. That makes them incredibly inadequate real-time performance feedback tools – like driving a car forwards with only the rear view mirror to go by – and it's for this reason that BPM experts refer to them as lagging indicators.

They lag where the business finds itself right now, and they definitely struggle – to the point of failing – to indicate how likely we are to be 'on plan' next quarter, or the quarter after that. Or how to quantify 'unlikely'. Or what might be done about it.

They have another weakness. Traditional financial accounting isn't a natural at representing intangible assets and capabilities, despite these frequently being pivotal to the modern organization.

The Balanced Scorecard perspectives

Kaplan and Norton, it appears, weren't content simply to recognize this. Rather, they dedicated themselves to finding complementary reports that might be called leading indicators, throwing a light on how critical aspects of an organization are performing right now and therefore belying how likely the money side of things might come good.

But while money is common currency to all businesses with common metrics, no other universal metrics spring to mind. There's no point in proposing a report called 'on-time deliveries' for example, which might work for a florist or parcel delivery company, but not a utility or a school. Or 'widgets in stock', which is a perfectly valid metric in organizations with factories and shops, but less so for a consultancy firm or telecommunications company.

Kaplan and Norton's first task was to identify other aspects of organizational life that were not only universal but proved to be powerful foci in directing operations, executing strategy and pursuing the vision. We have seen that metrics are too contextual to the nature of the business at hand to be universally relevant, so we need to go up a level so to speak. Kaplan and Norton developed four foci that are known as the Balanced Scorecard perspectives:

- *Financial* – to succeed financially, how should we appear to our shareholders?
- *Customer* – to achieve our vision, how should we appear to our customers?
- *Internal business processes* – to satisfy our shareholders and customers, what business processes must we excel at?
- *Learning and growth* – to achieve our vision, how will we sustain our ability to change and improve?

While the financial perspective remains an essential lagging indicator, we now have the opportunity with the three other leading indicator perspectives to ameliorate its weaknesses. The measures within the financial perspective are outcomes, and the measures within the other three perspectives are drivers.

Common questions at this juncture are: What about the other stakeholders? Why just a customer perspective? Table 6.1 portrays where the stakeholders are represented.

The next question typically raises the fact that almost all organizations already have non-financial performance metrics for essential business

Table 6.1: Stakeholder representation in the Balanced Scorecard perspectives

Perspective	Stakeholder representation
Financial	Shareholder
Customer	Customer; Prospect; Client
Internal processes	Partner
Learning and growth	Employee; Citizen; Netizen

functions; these are often referred to as key performance indicators (KPIs). So what's the difference? Significantly, the Balanced Scorecard fervently insists that non-financial metrics aren't designed at the coalface for matters that appear to be important at the coalface, but rather are determined by the diligent cascade down from the organization's vision and strategy. In other words, they are determined by what really is important and in harmony with all other metrics.

Objectives are set for each perspective that, if nothing else changes, should be wholly necessary and sufficient to result in the organization achieving its vision, or at least the overarching objectives set this year in pursuit of that vision: the objectives for each perspective guide metric selection, target setting and strategy formulation. Of course things do change in the operational environment, and such changes then demand adjustment of the overarching strategy and the objectives and strategies for each perspective and a re-cascade in order to keep the organization on track to deliver on its promises.

One of my favourite observations from the *Balanced Scorecard* book is that the authors had never come across a management team that had reached full consensus on the relative importance of its strategic objectives. They attribute this to executives' obsession with their own specialism and corresponding 'blind spots' when it comes to the other disciplines, and propose that the Balanced Scorecard helps to iron out such subjectivity. We'll return to this issue in the microcosm of marketing and PR, or more precisely the domain of the influence professional.

The right metrics

We've already encountered a couple of metrics in this book that failed to impress. The first was advertising value equivalence (AVE), presented for many years as the way to calculate the value of public relations campaigns. Yet if your organization or client has a spot of trouble in one quarter, demanding that you work your hardest to keep them out of the press, you are then working against the measure of your success. And what about all the other aspects of public relations beyond media relations? Shall we neglect them? Indeed, PR teams ended up doing just that, and I attribute this failure, this narrowing of the profession over the years, in part to the obsession with a seriously flawed metric that was designed (if that verb doesn't overemphasize a thought process that appears to have been lacking) and adopted without proper due diligence.

In my first week as industrial engineering manager at a manufacturing facility I was set the challenge of finding out why the warehouse was too often full of stuff we'd made but was not yet needed and short of the products that were needed. The answer lay in the metrics. How was the performance of each production shift, and therefore each shift manager, measured? It turned out that the sole metric was the rate at which the production lines ran. The metric was woefully inadequate in that it did not convey that making the right quantity of the right stuff at the right time was important to the business. It was inadequate because, while production rate is important, it cannot be the be all and end all.

I also learned something equally important on that job. We could have had this situation fixed in less than a week by taking people out of the equation, and yet it took seven months. Why? Because all metrics must be relevant and all relevant metrics must be visible, and all visible metrics are political.

Our business performance management review ended up being pivotal to the overall improvement to the business unit and won us *Management Today*'s Best Process Factory Award just two years later. (We were manufacturing to order by then and no longer needed to rent the warehouse at all – which is testament in part to the power of measuring the right things in the right way.)

We've also touched upon a typical call centre metric – calls per hour. When this metric stands alone or stands out, you know that someone in a sufficiently senior role does not appreciate the fact that people perform as they are measured. He or she did not check to see if the behaviour the metric catalysed was conducive to organizational success. Equally, no one likes to be on the phone to customer service for ever and a day, so what metric ensures that we get this right and ensures that we maximize the benefit to the customer and organization? We need a balance, and by definition no one metric can be balanced. For this reason, you can have a good stab at assessing whether a call centre is well run simply by seeking to understand its objectives and associated approach to metrics – its instigation of an appropriately balanced set of visible performance metrics.

Cause and effect

A well-designed metric must be visible to everyone whose behaviour it is designed to guide in an optimal way. This sounds obvious when you write it down, but sometimes you come across managers who like to keep these things tight to their chests. There must be, if you like, an individual cause and effect at play. The individual develops an affinity for the cause through the performance metrics, or at least his part in the bigger scheme of things, and the effect demanded of him. Often, just this clarification and new appreciation for his role and how he fits into the organization has a motivational benefit.

We're also looking for an organizational cause and effect. We're seeking via the Balanced Scorecard to achieve organizational coherence and coordination and effectiveness, and this becomes apparent as you look up through the perspectives. A properly constructed scorecard recognizes a chain of causes and effects that bind the four perspectives together. An acid test of a good Balanced Scorecard is that it should 'tell the story of the business unit's strategy',[91] and this idea is expanded further in strategy maps, as we shall see.

Kaplan and Norton consider there to be two kinds of feedback loop at play. Feedback about whether the planned strategy is being executed according to the plan is known as 'single loop learning', and feedback about whether the planned strategy remains a viable and successful strategy is known as 'double loop learning'. This is useful terminology for our later review of the Influence Scorecard.

The Balanced Scorecard is a powerful management tool. There are many more features, characteristics, qualities and implications of the Balanced Scorecard approach than I have space to discuss here, but I hope I have conveyed sufficient context to ground the next section on strategy maps, and then the Influence Scorecard.

Strategy maps

In the introduction to their book *Strategy Maps*,[92] Kaplan and Norton write:

> . . . the measurement system should focus on the entity's strategy – how it expects to create future, sustainable value. In designing Balanced

Scorecards, therefore, an organization must measure the critical few parameters that represent its strategy for long-term value creation.

. . . Without a comprehensive description of strategy, executives cannot easily communicate the strategy among themselves or to their employees. Without a shared understanding of the strategy, executives cannot create alignment around it. And, without alignment, executives cannot implement their new strategies . . .

And they summarize the purpose of strategy maps at the end of the second chapter:

The strategy map provides the visual framework for integrating the organization's objectives in the four perspectives of a Balanced Scorecard. It illustrates the cause-and-effect relationships that link desired outcomes in the customer and financial perspectives to outstanding performance in critical internal processes – operations management, customer management, innovation, and regulatory and social processes. These critical processes create and deliver the organization's value proposition to targeted customers and also promote the organization's productivity objectives in the financial perspective. Further, the strategy map identifies the specific capabilities in the organization's intangible assets – human capital, information capital, and organization capital – that are required for delivering exceptional performance in the critical internal processes.

It's worth mentioning that Kaplan and Norton base their work on Michael Porter's articulation of strategy – about selecting the set of activities in which an organization will excel to create a sustainable difference in the marketplace, and thereby creating sustained value for its shareholders (or sustainable value in the case of non-profits).

And for the sake of clarity, let's expand on what's encompassed by those different forms of 'capital' referred to above:

- *Human capital* – skills, knowledge and values
- *Information capital* – systems, databases, networks
- *Organization capital* – culture, leadership, alignment, teamwork.

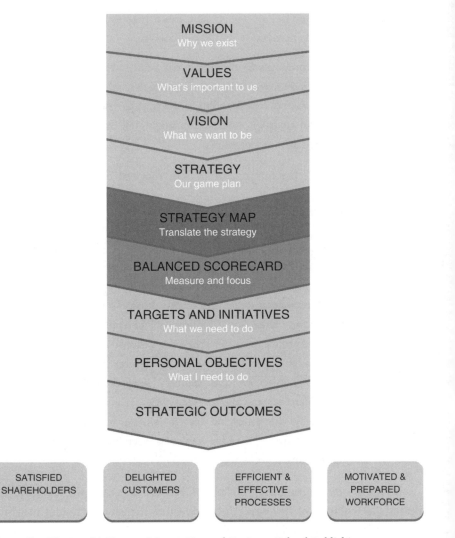

Figure 6.1: The 'stack' (*Strategy Maps* © Harvard Business School Publishing 2004, reproduced with permission)

Figure 6.1 shows the contribution that strategy maps and the Balanced Scorecard make in the scheme of things – where they fit in the 'stack'.

Figure 6.2 portrays the generic strategy map that has clearly evolved from the four perspectives of the Balanced Scorecard. The arrows indicate cause and effect over time, and each perspective is examined in more detail offering

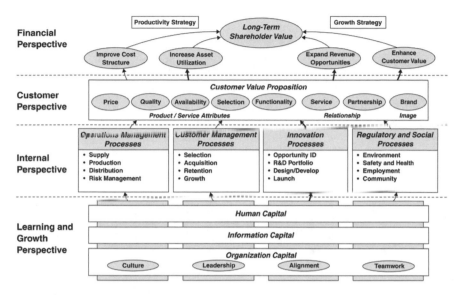

Figure 6.2: A strategy map represents how the organization creates value. (*Strategy Maps* © Harvard Business School Publishing 2004, reproduced with permission)

up a normative checklist of a strategy's components and interrelationships. Indeed, Kaplan and Norton go so far as to say that if your strategy fails to address an element in this figure then it is probably flawed. In other words, the strategy mapping process is often so demanding, in a constructive way, that it prompts an immediate review of the strategy definition phase.

Figure 6.2 is the helicopter view, and Kaplan and Norton show how you can 'zoom in', so to speak, on any element.

Table 6.2, for example, zooms in on the four bullets shown in the customer management processes box of Figure 6.2, expanding them into four columns. Each column then shows the internal perspective (the processes to excel at to satisfy customers and stakeholders) and the learning and growth perspectives (how to sustain the ability to change and improve to achieve the vision) across each type of capital: human, information and organization. Table 6.3 shows the typical management processes Kaplan and Norton identify for four process families within the internal perspective.

As you might suspect, developing a comprehensive strategy, mapping it and then designing and maintaining the corresponding Balanced Scorecard isn't a simple task that you can start during morning coffee and complete in

Table 6.2: Learning and growth strategies for customer management. (*Strategy Maps*, © Harvard Business School Publishing 2004, reproduced with permission)

The customer management processes –		Customer selection	Customer acquisition	Customer retention	Customer growth
Internal perspective	**Processes**	▪ Understand segments ▪ Screen unprofitable customers ▪ Target high-value customers ▪ Manage the brand	▪ Communicate value proposition ▪ Customize mass marketing ▪ Acquire / convert leads ▪ Develop dealer network	▪ Premium customer service ▪ 'Sole source' partnerships ▪ Service excellence ▪ Lifetime customers	▪ Cross-selling ▪ Solution selling ▪ Partnering / integrated management ▪ Customer education
Learning and growth perspective	**Human capital**	▪ Market research ▪ Profitability analysis ▪ Market communication	▪ Market research ▪ Profitability analysis ▪ Market communication	▪ Call centre protocols ▪ Product line knowledge ▪ Problem resolution ▪ Customer feedback	▪ Consultative sales skills ▪ Customer / industry knowledge ▪ Product line knowledge
	Information capital	▪ Customer database ▪ Customer analytics ▪ E-polling / sampling ▪ Profitability analysis	▪ Database marketing ▪ Lead management ▪ Sales force automation ▪ Website design	▪ Customer interaction centre ▪ Problem tracking system ▪ Order management system	▪ Customer information feedback ▪ Portfolio planning models ▪ Integrated order management
	Organization capital	▪ Customer-focused culture ▪ Personal goal alignment ▪ Best-practice sharing	▪ Customer-focused culture ▪ Personal goal alignment ▪ Best-practice sharing	▪ Customer-focused culture ▪ Personal goal alignment ▪ Best-practice sharing	▪ Customer-focused culture ▪ Personal goal alignment ▪ Best-practice sharing

Table 6.3: Example management processes listed in *Strategy Maps* for the four internal perspectives

Internal perspective –	Operations management processes	Customer management processes	Innovation processes	Regulatory and social processes
Management processes	**Develop supplier relationships** ■ Lower cost of ownership ■ Just-in-time delivery ■ High-quality supply ■ New ideas from suppliers ■ Supplier partnerships ■ Outsource mature non-strategic sources	**Customer selection** ■ Understand segments ■ Screen unprofitable customers ■ Target high-value customers ■ Manage the brand	**Identify the opportunities** ■ Anticipate customer needs ■ Discover new opportunities	**Environment** ■ Energy and resource consumption ■ Water and air emissions ■ Solid waste disposal ■ Product environmental impact
	Produce products and services ■ Lower cost of production ■ Continuous improvement ■ Process cycle time ■ Fixed asset utilization ■ Working capital efficiency	**Customer acquisition** ■ Communicate value proposition ■ Customize mass marketing ■ Acquire / convert leads ■ Develop dealer network	**Manage the portfolio** ■ Choose and manage mix of projects ■ Extend products to new applications ■ Collaborate	**Safety and health** ■ Safety ■ Health
	Distribute to customers ■ Lower cost to serve ■ Responsive delivery time ■ Enhance quality	**Customer retention** ■ Premium customer service ■ 'Sole source' partnerships ■ Service excellence ■ Lifetime customers	**Design and develop** ■ Manage products through development stages ■ Reduce development cycle time ■ Reduce development costs	**Employment** ■ Diversity ■ Employ the unemployable
	Manage risk ■ Financial risk (high credit rating) ■ Operating risk ■ Technological risk	**Customer growth** ■ Cross-selling ■ Solution selling ■ Partnering / integrated management ■ Customer education	**Launch** ■ Ramp-up time ■ Production cost, quality, cycle time ■ Achieve initial sales goals	**Community** ■ Community programmes ■ Alliances with non-profits

time for afternoon tea. Every organization is unique, every business unit is unique, every business unit's strategy is unique, and every business unit's strategy map and Balanced Scorecard is unique. BPM consultants and in-house specialists make it their job to get to grips with the strategy maps and Balanced Scorecard processes and their continued honing.

In *The Execution Premium*,[93] Kaplan and Norton present a six-stage, closed-loop management process:

1. *Define the strategy* – mission, values, vision, strategic analysis and formulation
2. *Plan and translate the strategy* – with strategy maps and Balanced Scorecards
3. *Align the organization* – with cascading linked strategy maps and Balanced Scorecards, to team and employee personal objectives and incentives
4. *Link to operational processes* – plan how operations should run to execute the strategy
5. *Monitor and learn* – management review meetings focused on problems, barriers and challenges
6. *Test and adapt the strategy* – apply the knowledge accrued in the context of the changing operational environment and emerging strategies to prepare to recommence this loop.

As you will imagine, Kaplan and Norton practise what they preach. Their own ongoing closed-loop management process is focused on the execution and performance of their frameworks in the field. When reality has fallen short of expectations, they've studied the reasons and adjusted or augmented their recommendations accordingly; indeed they frequently credit such work in their books.

Kaplan and Norton have paid particular attention to the ownership of the strategy mapping and Balanced Scorecard processes. It has been recognized that the nature of the task at hand is so integral to an organization as to basically define it – so outsourcing the processes here to external consultants is the first step on the road to failure. Such outside consultancies may be valuable to guide the process, to establish momentum quickly and increase the likelihood of a successful rollout, but ownership must lie squarely within the organization.

In *The Execution Premium*, Kaplan and Norton discuss theme owners – that is, members of the executive team who are given 'night jobs' overseeing the execution of assigned strategic themes in addition to their day jobs as functional heads or heads of business. They also expand on the emergence in the field of what they labelled in a 2005 paper[94] the office of strategy management, or OSM for short.

Office of strategy management

Kaplan and Norton differentiate the OSM in the paper from the traditional strategic planning unit as follows:

> The typical planning function facilitates the annual strategic planning process but takes little or no leadership role in seeing that the strategy gets executed. The companies we studied, however, recognize that effective strategy execution requires communicating corporate strategy; ensuring that enterprise-level plans are translated into the plans of the various units and departments; executing strategic initiatives to deliver on the grand plan; and aligning employees' competency development plans, and the personal goals and incentives, with strategic objectives. What's more, they recognize that the company's strategy must be tested and adapted to stay abreast of the changing competition. The OSM becomes the central point for coordinating all these tasks. It does not do all the work, but it facilitates the processes so that strategy execution gets accomplished in an integrated fashion across the enterprise.

The OSM is a response to the fact that in traditional organizational structures no functional head existed with the responsibility for strategy. Kaplan and Norton continued to work with OSM working groups after they published their paper and then, in writing *The Execution Premium*, they were able to flesh out the roles and responsibilities of the OSM more exactly. The first two roles are the responsibility of full-time OSM staff, and the third pulls the appropriate functional heads into the process.

- *Architect*
  - Define the strategy management framework and conventions

- ○ Design the strategy management process
- ■ *Process owner*
  - ○ Develop the strategy
  - ○ Plan the strategy
  - ○ Align the organization
  - ○ Review and adapt the strategy
- ■ *Integrator*
  - ○ Link to operational planning/budgeting (CFO)
  - ○ Link to key operating processes (COO)
  - ○ Link to HR, IT, and support functions (HRO, CIO)
  - ○ Communicate strategy (Head of Corporate Communications)
  - ○ Manage strategic initiatives (programme management)
  - ○ Share best practices (Chief Knowledge Officer).

A typical OSM of a large company requires six to eight staff, and it helps if it reports directly to the CEO. Sometimes the OSM takes the form of a centralized corporate office, and sometimes just one or two persons serve at the corporate staff level with the remainder of the team made up from a network of individuals across the business.

Of interest, and another facet we'll return to again later in the context of the Influence Scorecard, is the role the OSM has in not just doing the right things but making sure the organization doesn't get distracted doing the wrong things, or at least things that aren't strategic priorities. It's obvious that investments should be made in projects that have total strategic alignment rather than the stuff that, while appearing to make sense at the coalface, is not aligned. When Marriott Vacation Club International instituted an OSM in 2002 it soon found itself embarking on a 'kill the initiative campaign' to streamline what the business was focused on.[95] This can be difficult in terms of nurturing and maintaining motivation for the new (strategically aligned) initiatives after you just discarded the last project mid-way, but it also answers the attack from detractors that they have no more bandwidth for yet another programme. And ultimately it comes down to whether you want strategic alignment now, or later.

Return on investment

Here are some quick examples of when the pursuits of ROI or decisions made in the name of ROI become farcical. I'm sure many readers will have come across such situations.

- *When the boss rules* – 'Look, I'm told we're investing in this. Now we just need to work up the numbers to get it through finance.'
- *When efficiency rules* – 'This investment will speed the process up.' 'Er, but it's not actually a bottleneck.'
- *When the guru rules* – 'Well the book's at number 1.'
- *When last year rules* – 'Well we did it this way last year . . .'
- *When the competition rules* – 'They've gone for it, so. . . .'
- *When vanity rules* – 'We can afford it and it'll be a testament to our time.'
- *When experience rules* – 'Do you think the CMO's background in advertising sways the budgeting process?'
- *When rules rule* – 'Let's treat it as three separate projects so each comes under the limit demanding cost justification.'
- *When paralysis rules* – 'I just don't know.'

And when all else fails:

- *When cost rules* – 'Just make a decision on a least-cost basis because this sort of thing never has a tangible ROI.'

Arguably the most significant advantage of strategy maps and the OSM's dedication to the task is a clearer understanding of return on investment. When strategy rules.

You'll recall that the financial perspective is the outcome, and the customer, internal processes, and learning and growth perspectives are drivers. You'll also recall that the strategy mapping and Balanced Scorecarding work establishes a cause and effect:

- We need to improve our ability to operate in the way we've identified in order to delight the customer and subsequently the shareholders; and
- We need to build our human, information and organizational capital this particular way in order to excel at those processes.

Here, then, are the aspects of the business to invest in, and, by disassociation, the aspects not to invest in. Or, in other words, executing against the strategy map and Balanced Scorecard has ROI built in by design. Here's how Kaplan and Norton put it in *Strategy Maps* in relation to traditionally the most difficult investments to justify, intangibles:

> Economic justification of these strategic investments can be performed, but not in traditional ways. The common approach is on a stand-alone basis: 'Show the ROI of the new IT application', or 'Demonstrate the payback from the HR training program.' . . . But each investment or initiative is only one ingredient in the bigger recipe. Each is necessary, but not sufficient. Economic justification is determined by evaluating the return from the entire portfolio of investments in intangible assets that will deliver the ROI from [the strategic imperative].

Back to influence

I'll keep you no longer from getting back to the topic at hand: *influence*. I have presented all I think is needed to set the groundwork for the Influence Scorecard. I'll finish here with one last quote from another section of the Kaplan and Norton paper we referenced earlier. It offers a pertinent insight from a practitioner and provides the most perfect segue from Balanced Scorecard to Influence Scorecard.

Graham Sher is the CEO of Canadian Blood Services based in Ottawa, the non-profit charitable organization that looks after the supply of blood and blood products for Canadians, and he contributed a section of the paper describing his reasons for adopting the Balanced Scorecard and instituting an OSM:

> . . . while many people believe that chief executives wield direct and easy influence, the reality is that any CEO has a difficult time influencing his or her organization. A CEO's attempts to command and control undermine the authority of senior executives. I want to exert my influence indirectly and in a way that empowers my executives and creates an environment in which they can lead and manage their parts of the organization.

Summary

- People perform as they are measured.
- Measurement is an active, dynamic management tool as well as a feedback mechanism.
- The Balanced Scorecard transforms an organization's strategic plan from an attractive but passive document into the 'marching orders' for the organization on a daily basis.
- Financial reports describe outcomes, but are lagging indicators of business performance.
- Kaplan and Norton identified three perspectives of business performance as leading indicators and drivers of the business outcomes – the customer perspective, the internal processes perspective, and the learning and growth perspective.
- Non-financial metrics aren't designed at the coalface for matters that appear to be important at the coalface, but rather are determined by the diligent cascade down from the organization's vision and strategy.
- All metrics must be relevant, all relevant metrics must be visible, and all visible metrics are political.
- We need balance, and by definition no one metric can be balanced.
- Cause-and-effect must be visible – a good Balanced Scorecard tells the story of the business unit's strategy.
- Strategy must be well described and communicated to secure appropriate organizational alignment.
- The strategy map provides the visual framework for integrating the organization's objectives into the four perspectives of a Balanced Scorecard.
- Intangible assets are described in terms of human, information and organization capital.
- An outsourced Balanced Scorecard is a failed Balanced Scorecard – it must be owned by the organization.
- The office of strategy management owns strategy formulation, communication, translation and alignment.
- Executing against the strategy map and Balanced Scorecard has ROI built in by design.

It is now time to meet the Influence Scorecard.

7

If you're in business, you're in the business of influence. And when it comes to looking at the business of influence we formed the Six Influence Flows from a deliberately carte blanche starting point, devoid of the baggage and blinkers of traditional terminology, demarcations, expectations, interpretations and misinterpretations. Every organization must exert influence and be influenced.

This could entail paying for the right media space. It might involve identifying who might be effective intermediaries. It could be servicing customers' needs in a particular way. It could demand particular sensitivity to conversations your customers and prospects are having with a competitor. It could be opportunities to get your message over on the street. It might require getting the right mix of people mixing. It could be some insightful, poignant or entertaining content that's too irresistible to the right audience not to discuss and share.

It could be the sights, sounds and smells in-store. It might be the most timely and targeted market research. It might require an innovative promotion. It could be the little addition to the proposition the customer wasn't expecting. It could be your earnest adoption of renewable energy sources. It could be your willingness to engage stakeholders in public and private conversations.

It *could be* some or all these things, and many other things. Now let's describe what it *will be*.

It will be your definition of your influence objectives in the light of your values.

It will be the crystallization of your influence strategy, the set of influence activities in which you must excel in order to create a sustainable difference in the marketplace.

It will be the way you map the influence strategy into the fabric of the organization.

It will be your identification of the most critical corresponding components of your human, information and organizational capital, and how they must be enhanced.

It will be the identification of appropriate metrics and the construction of a Balanced Scorecard or similar BPM approach.

It will be the corresponding alignment of the organization – structurally and culturally – through the communication of the strategy, causes and effects and metrics.

It will be everyone in the organization recognizing their contribution to influencing and being influenced, and living up to the organization's and their own expectations accordingly. Performing as they are measured. Performing because it feels right.

The Balanced Scorecard and the Influence Scorecard

I need to clarify what the Influence Scorecard is exactly. In fact, like the Balanced Scorecard after which it is named, I find myself using it in two contexts.

Firstly, there is the act of setting measures, targets and reporting. As we'll explore further in this chapter, the Influence Scorecard underlines the importance of identifying measurement criteria and tracing influence, and the actual ongoing acts of measurement and single- and double-loop learning. It represents all the differentiated influence processes for incorporation into business performance management (BPM), the Balanced Scorecard or other method of choice. The Influence Scorecard is then simply a subset or view of the Balanced Scorecard containing all the influence-related KPIs stripped of functional silo, and it may extend beyond the Balanced Scorecard should a greater operational granularity of metrics be demanded by the influence strategy than is required to be reported to general business management. This one comprehensive view on influence helps to ensure that the full potential to influence and be influenced is exploited cohesively and consistently.

Secondly, there is the philosophy and management approach. The Influence Scorecard is the name of our influence framework and our management approach to setting influence strategy within the purview of the Six Influence Flows and mapping influence strategy. Working with the Influence Scorecard, one cannot help but throw a new light on the influence processes that permeate the entire organization and not just those within the functional areas known as marketing and PR. And this new light might seed the opportunity to revise the structure, culture and processes of the organization to improve its capabilities in executing the influence strategy, its differentiated influence processes. It holds the promise of unlocking the potential that integrated marketing communications always sought, and with organization-wide implications, not just in the marcoms domain.

In both regards it is part of – and an augmentation to – the Balanced Scorecard (or similar BPM approach). It cannot exist in isolation. The Influence Scorecard can only thrive in organizations that are already practising business performance management effectively. It needs the cause-and-effect linkages to be mapped and well understood in order to de-politicize budgeting and measurement, to enable organizational learning, and to put the ROI question finally to bed.

One might ask why our focus here couldn't be represented as a strategy that maps into the Balanced Scorecard, just like other strategies. Why give this view on / augmentation of the Balanced Scorecard its own name? Quite simply, the Six Influence Flows is not a strategy; it represents a completely new take on the influence processes that are manifestly disparate, siloed and largely uncoordinated today, and, unlike a strategy, this new take applies to all organizations without exception. Moreover, and more ambitiously, the term 'Balanced Scorecard' has become synonymous with its underlying BPM philosophy, and I see 'Influence Scorecard' as synonymous with ours. Either way, it's the opportunity to put influence at the centre of organizational strategy that's important, not the phraseology.

I hope it goes without saying that influence must be represented in the boardroom, otherwise what is an organization without it? The Influence

Scorecard secures the Chief Influence Officer a seat at the table – an outcome we'll return to later.

Taking a lead

The two most memorable quotes from probably the most famous leadership expert, Professor Warren Bennis, are[96]:

> Leaders are people who do the right thing; managers are people who do things right. Both roles are crucial, but they differ profoundly. I often observe people in top positions doing the wrong things well.

And:

> The manager asks how and when; the leader asks what and why.

I see Influence Performance Management as a subset of Business Performance Management, but before we get to the management aspects let's explore some of the ways our influence framework presents real opportunities for leadership. Taking the time to look at influence processes afresh prompts many questions that begin with what and why, for example and in no particular order:

- Why is there too often a tension between marketing and PR; or worse, silence?
- What is the point of questioning who 'owns' social media / SEO / social commerce / content, etc. – a debate that has consumed considerable attention and energy?
- Why is customer service so separate from marketing and PR?
- What's it like to be one of our stakeholders, being influenced by us, being influenced by our competitors? And do they think they influence us?
- Why do most PR consultants invest considerably more time getting the message out than getting the message in (or are directed as such)?

- Why are those people who talk most often to customers and prospects less involved in product innovation and development than those who talk to such stakeholders less often?
- Why do last year's budget, who-shouts-loudest and the CMO's gut feelings hold so much sway over the budgeting process?
- Why does it feel as if we're fluttering from one hot trend to the next without deriving value? Or: Why aren't we on the front foot in knowing how to respond to the next big thing, how it fits to our strategy and ethos?
- Why does everyone know that our human, information and organization capital aren't quite fit for purpose as far as influence is concerned, but no one knows what to do about it?
- What if strategy was grounded in the organization's vision rather than in functional / departmental definitions?
- If our strategy is unique and therefore our differentiated processes are unique, why does our organizational structure pivot around the same discipline-oriented departments as everyone else? Shouldn't the structure be fit-for-process?

Influence objectives

Some texts present objectives as an output of strategic planning; a list of things the specified strategy insists must get done. However, I'm using objectives here in the context of a precursor to strategy formulation. We have the organization's vision (a statement about where we want to be) and the organization's goals (the broad and general statements about how to get there). Objectives are more narrowly but more precisely defined than goals, describing the 'what' so that we might then formulate the strategy – the 'how'.

I said that influence was the task at hand in Chapter 3, before then discussing example outcomes:

- Reputation
- Trust
- Significance
- Purchases
- Expressions of preference or support

- Other actions we want to instil (engagement)
- And greater insight into and articulation of our stakeholders' situations, needs and desires.

These are example objectives of influencing and being influenced.

The Chief Influence Officer and team will form the organization's specific influence objectives from the organization's mission, values and vision. The mission (why the organization exists) identifies the customers the organization exists to serve and what exactly it exists to do for them. The values (what's important to the organization) distinguish between those influence activities that are desirable and those that are unacceptable. And the vision (what the organization wants to be) informs the objectives for the organization, the attainment of which will take it from where it is today to where it wants to be. Each overarching organizational objective may demand a subset of influence objectives that are wholly necessary and sufficient in influence terms to accomplish the overarching objective.

For each organizational objective, the influence objectives will then refer to each stakeholder group in terms of each of the Six Influence Flows as relevant.

Table 7.1 portrays an influence objectives matrix that can be deployed for the whole organization or strategic business unit (SBU).

Table 7.1: Influence objectives matrix

Organizational objective	Customers	Suppliers	Etc.
1st flow (our influence with our stakeholders)	Influence objectives	Influence objectives	
2nd flow (our stakeholders' influence with each other in respect to us)	Influence objectives	Influence objectives	
3rd flow (our stakeholders' influence with us)	Influence objectives	Influence objectives	
4th flow (our competitors' influence with our stakeholders)	Influence objectives	Influence objectives	
5th flow (our stakeholders' influence with each other in respect to our competitors)	Influence objectives	Influence objectives	
6th flow (our stakeholders' influence with our competitors)	Influence objectives	Influence objectives	

Is it appropriate to cascade the influence objectives matrix down to the brand level or product line? In my opinion the board should already have addressed this in the formation of SBUs. According to the Balanced Scorecard Institute,[97] a SBU is a unit of the company that has a separate mission and objectives, and can be planned and evaluated independently from the other parts of the company. A SBU may be a division, a product line or an individual brand. When you consider that influence objectives will inform the influence strategy and ultimately the team and individual behaviour, it's unrealistic to ask any individual to behave favourably in the first instance towards brand X then suddenly switch to brand Y. If X and Y are so different they should be contained in separate SBUs. Therefore, influence objectives should be expressed at the SBU level, and if this doesn't end up feeling right, then perhaps the board needs to review its overall organizational structure.

We may then have augmented the definition of a SBU as being an entity with one universal set of influence objectives.

The Six Influence Flows framework forces the removal of blinkers that are too easily donned when setting marketing objectives or PR objectives for example. The Six Influence Flows are media agnostic and there are no preconceived discipline-oriented ideas. We don't ask: 'What's our advertising objective?' We don't even ask: 'Should we advertise?' or 'Do we need a media relations campaign?' And we definitely don't forget the influence roles being played elsewhere in the business, in packaging design, in customer service, by retail staff, in environmental management and in HR, for example. Indeed, given the familiarity that most of us have with the typical functions within a typical organization, it may well prove to be helpful in so much as representing a mental tick list when setting influence objectives, e.g. 'What influence activities must we encourage in accounts receivable / transport / procurement?' Nevertheless, care should also be taken to ensure that such a tick list does not limit thoroughness (we've already discussed the shortcomings of functional thinking). Another way to consider influence objectives is via mapping the customer journey and exploring the influence touch points of such a journey. This well-known concept should then be extended to the supplier journey, reseller journey, employee journey, etc.

We avoid building in the fragmentation and potential for disjointedness one sees repeatedly in objectives setting. We avoid reinforcing siloed thinking. Rather, we simply describe the influence we're intent on making happen, and the influence objectives then drive the formulation of the influence strategy.

Influence strategy

I referred earlier to one of my favourite observations from the *Balanced Scorecard* book in which the authors state that they had never come across a management team that had reached full consensus on the relative importance of its strategic objectives; and they attribute this to executives' obsession with their own specialism and corresponding 'blind spots' when it comes to the other disciplines. In my experience, this applies equally among the leaders of the marketing and PR teams. We've just seen how setting influence objectives rather than marketing objectives and PR objectives opens out the scope of the work; it distances it from each participant's comfort zone or rut. This advantage continues with the development of influence strategy.

The influence strategy is at once part of the overall organizational strategy (for what is an organizational strategy devoid of any aspect of influence?) and driven by it (see Figure 7.1).

An organization's strategy describes how it expects to create future, sustainable value for all its stakeholders. Its influence strategy describes how it expects to influence and be influenced in ways that are wholly necessary and sufficient for the achievement of the influence objectives and successful execution of the overarching strategy.

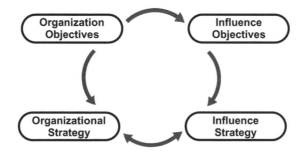

Figure 7.1: Objectives and strategy

The influence strategy is the set of influence activities in which you must excel in order to help to create a sustainable difference in the marketplace. It facilitates organizational coherence, coordination and effectiveness of influence.

The CMO's dilemma

John Bell heads up Ogilvy PR's global digital practice. In a paper titled *Socialize the Enterprise,*[98] July 2010, John calls for a 'comprehensive social media strategy' and identifies what he refers to in a corresponding blog post as the CMO's dilemma. It goes like this:

> After a year of experimentation in social media, the CMO of a global Fast Moving Consumer Goods (FMCG) company realized that, once again, his team's latest effort was not working. He was frustrated. This time, he thought, they had cracked it. From the outset, the team looked to existing agency partners and new social media gurus to help them to tack the social media programs to their product campaigns. The media companies offered paid placements in social networks. The advertising creatives designed a clever Facebook application, and the public relations team suggested reaching out to some bloggers to spread word of mouth. The brand team felt they had the tactics to transform their traditional marketing campaign into a social media campaign. But, with no real way to measure the impact of blog posts, Tweets or the limited use of the Facebook application, it just seemed like a lot of work to generate modest word of mouth online. Where was the ROI in that? When the three-month campaign came to a close, the CMO was disappointed. He wanted something bigger, something that reminded him of mass media.

Many readers will recognize such a dilemma, and we'll return to the ROI aspect later in this chapter. The paper is a very worthwhile read. It addresses training and organization (as we have done in this text) with respect to the strategy map's intangible assets – human and organization capital. It doesn't refer to information capital, but I know from talking with John that Ogilvy PR gets the technology side of things, as you'd expect. I'm less comfortable with the paper's apparent isolation of social media from the rest of the world of influence, but I imagine that will have been the result of the paper's scope rather than any conscious separation.

On that point, however, I do wonder when the emphasis on 'social' this and 'digital' that might finally die. The fact that Ogilvy PR has a 'digital practice' isn't shocking per se – after all, many advertising and PR firms have similarly named teams – but surely it must become a less and less relevant distinction with each year's passing. In that respect, I recall a conversation with a PR industry leader on this subject in 2007. In reply to my assertion that having a digital practice or service was ridiculous, given that digital wasn't a standalone service but permeated everything a marketing and PR consultancy should be about, I was told: 'Ah yes, but that's what people buy.' I had no response, and left knowing that I had just been given a sharp lesson in marketing. Perhaps this book might begin to change people's procurement approach, so we shall review that in more detail later.

The most salient sentence in *Socialize the Enterprise*'s conclusion to our focus here is:

> Only a company-wide strategic approach that puts social media at the center of brand strategy, accrues useful learning and applies meaningful new measurement tools will produce the kind of results marketers need and consumers want.

Perhaps we might take this, broaden it and reframe it to our structure. Only an organization-wide strategic approach that (a) puts influence at the centre of organizational strategy, (b) enables single- and double-loop learning, and (c) applies a Balanced Scorecard type approach will produce the results that the board and influence professionals need and that all stakeholders want.

The CMO's dilemma has been resolved, and in fact we may have begun to define the role of the Chief Influence Officer, but more on that later.

Mapping the influence strategy

You have identified your influence objectives and the set of influence activities in which you must excel in order to help to create a sustainable difference in the marketplace – the influence strategy. It's now time to map it to visualize and communicate the causes and effects, to check its completeness, and to identify the required investment in intangible assets – i.e. human, information and organization capital.

It's worth restating briefly why dealing with these intangible assets in a professional manner is difficult, to the point of impossibility, without this kind of approach. The value derived from intangible assets is indirect, resulting only through chains of cause and effect; an intangible asset only has value in context, depending on its strategic alignment; intangible assets have to work together in harmony (referred to as bundles by Kaplan and Norton), rarely being valuable alone; and the cost of an intangible asset seldom has any relation to its value. Is it any wonder that investment in intangible assets causes such confusion and emotional debate?

Earlier, in Table 6.3, we listed example management processes found in *Strategy Maps* for the four internal perspectives: operations management processes, customer management processes, innovation processes, and regulatory and social processes. (Note that this 'social' is not the same 'social' as in 'social media'.) Now we can reproduce this table, keeping only those management processes that relate to influence and adding some other example influence processes (Table 7.2). For those entrenched in marketing and PR, an article in *McKinsey Quarterly* titled *Inventing the 21st-century purchasing organization*,[99] reminds us why our influence framework is powerful in giving us the first comprehensive view of all influence processes:

> Suppliers have always provided critical fuel for innovation – serving, for example, as a potential source of valuable insights and technologies that support product and process improvements. Purchasers serve as a fundamental link between a company's supply base and the rest of its value chain. Some companies exploit this connection quite effectively.

I have indicated in brackets the primary influence flows that each process involves. And, as we saw in Figure 6.2 and Table 6.2, we can drop down from the internal processes perspective to the learning and growth perspective's intangible assets (Table 7.3).

Table 7.2: Example influence management processes for the four internal perspectives

Internal perspective –	Operations management processes	Customer management processes	Innovation processes	Regulatory and social processes
Influence management processes	**Develop supplier relationships** ■ New ideas from suppliers (3rd) ■ Supplier partnerships (1st and 3rd) ■ Share customer insights with suppliers (3rd) **Produce products and services** ■ Offer early trials to fans (1st and 3rd) to identify production issues early	**Customer selection** ■ Understand segments (3rd) ■ Join the conversation to facilitate customer self-selection (1st and 3rd) **Customer acquisition** ■ Gather intelligence regarding competing products and services (4th, 5th and 6th) ■ Communicate value proposition (1st) ■ Customize mass marketing (1st) ■ Develop dealer network (1st and 3rd) ■ Responsive pre-sales support (1st and 3rd)	**Identify the opportunities** ■ Anticipate customer needs (3rd) ■ Discover new opportunities (3rd) ■ Listen, analyse and synthesize (3rd) ■ Crowd source ideas (1st and 3rd) ■ Trend spotting (3rd) **Manage the portfolio** ■ Collaborate (1st and 3rd) ■ Encourage customer mash-ups / re-engineering (1st and 2nd) ■ Gather intelligence regarding competing products and services (4th, 5th and 6th)	**Environment** ■ Transparent communication (public information) of environmental initiatives and performance (1st) ■ Crowd source ideas (3rd) **Safety and health** ■ Transparent communication (public information) of health and safety initiatives and performance, including supply chain (1st)

Distribute to customers

- Invite new customers to give feedback – opportunity to start a relationship (1st and 3rd)
- Gather intelligence regarding competing products and service distribution (4th, 5th and 6th)

Manage risk

- Monitor for the early signals of reputation risk – by stakeholder, including the netizens (2nd)
- Monitor for risks to competitors for potential exploitation (5th)

Customer retention

- Premium customer service (1st)
- Service excellence (1st)
- Lifetime customers (1st and 2nd)
- Community building (1st, 2nd and 3rd)
- Sensitize to early signals of retention problems (2nd and 3rd influence flows (our stakeholders' influence with us))

Customer growth

- Cross-selling (1st)
- Solution selling (1st)
- Partnering / integrated management (1st and 3rd)
- Customer education (1st)
- Focus on the influenced (1st, 2nd and 3rd)
- Influence tracing

Design and develop

- Manage products through development stages with close customer involvement (3rd)
- Reduce development cycle time with close customer involvement (3rd)

Launch

- Make fans integral; help fans make themselves integral (1st, 2nd and 3rd)

Employment

- Transparent communication (public information) of diversity and employment policies and performance (1st)

Community

- Open communication and engagement with local communities and non-profits (1st)

Grey text – processes carried over from *Strategy Maps*

Black text – additional processes to those listed in *Strategy Maps*

Brackets – indicate relevant influence flows

109

Table 7.3: Example intangible capital items / potential strategic foci in the learning and growth perspective

Internal perspective –		Operations and customer management processes	Innovation processes	Regulatory and social processes
Learning and growth perspective	Human capital	■ Balanced Scorecarding ■ Influence Scorecarding ■ Supplier management ■ Customer account management ■ Business intelligence ■ Marketing ■ Advertising ■ Public relations ■ Media relations ■ Investor relations ■ Internal comms ■ Social media ■ Web design & SEO ■ Branded apps and widgets ■ Copywriting and content ■ Branding ■ Graphic design ■ Packaging ■ Merchandising ■ Direct marketing ■ Publicity ■ Events and entertainment ■ Sponsorship	■ Customer service ■ Brand journalism ■ Promotion ■ Sales and sales promotion ■ Marketing and market research ■ Call centre protocols ■ Product line knowledge for pre-sales, sales and post-sales support ■ Consultative sales skills ■ Problem resolution ■ Customer feedback ■ Customer / industry knowledge ■ Analytical skills to collate, analyse and interpret the 3rd flow (our stakeholders' influence with us) ■ Analytical skills to collate, analyse and interpret all the other flows ■ Etc.	■ Product and service design and development ■ Outsourced R&D ■ Partner collaboration ■ Analytical skills to collate, analyse and interpret the 3rd flow (our stakeholders' influence with us) ■ Analytical skills to collate, analyse and interpret all the other flows ■ Focus group management	■ Public affairs ■ Public relations ■ Human resources ■ H&S expertise

Information capital	▪ Technology that facilitates influence flow monitoring and analysis and organizational learning ▪ Technology that facilitates Balanced Scorecarding ▪ Technology that facilitates Influence Scorecarding	▪ Social Web analytics ▪ Technology that facilitates focus on the influenced ▪ Technology that facilitates tracing influence ▪ Customer database ▪ Customer / retail analytics ▪ Marketing research ▪ Database marketing ▪ Lead management ▪ Sales force automation ▪ Website design ▪ Content management ▪ Customer interaction centre ▪ Problem tracking system ▪ Order management system ▪ Customer information feedback ▪ Integrated order management	▪ Technology to explore, integrate, and achieve speed to market ▪ Collaborative technologies	▪ Technology to aid collation and communication of data relating to environment, health and safety, employment, and community
Organization capital	▪ Influence-focused culture ▪ Personal goal alignment ▪ A culture that recognizes there's influence in everything ▪ A quality (TQM) focus	▪ Influence-focused culture ▪ Personal goal alignment ▪ A culture that recognizes there's influence in everything ▪ A culture of customer focus	▪ Influence-focused culture ▪ Personal goal alignment ▪ A culture that recognizes there's influence in everything ▪ A culture of innovation and continuous improvement	▪ Influence-focused culture ▪ Personal goal alignment ▪ A culture that recognizes there's influence in everything ▪ A culture of social awareness and responsibility

I have referred, in the human capital row, to those traditional terms we have tried hard so far to leave behind, such as 'advertising' and 'public relations'. But that's not a problem. There's no point in trying to concoct a new name for advertising skills if you've concluded in the influence strategy that advertising is what you need. Talking about skills in terms of '1st flow consumer targeted influence via paid media' doesn't quite have the same ring to it, and you might attract less applicants for the role! The inclusion of more traditional terms has no impact on the design or accomplishment of our strategic process.

I'm also aware that some of the terms overlap – for example, investor relations as a specialism of public relations – but the list is intended simply as a prompt for the type of skills that might be needed and doesn't purport to be a new taxonomy of influence professions.

Also, as all facets of organizational life entail some influence aspects, as there's influence in everything, the distinction of 'human capital' employed in operations as opposed to customer management processes becomes awkward or arbitrary. I've therefore taken the easy route and merged the respective cells of the table – although I'm not sure what Kaplan and Norton might have to say about it.

The Influence Scorecard and OSM

You'll recall that the creation of an office of strategy management is an increasingly common response in organizations seeking to increase the effectiveness with which they coordinate the communication of corporate strategy, the execution of strategic initiatives, and organizational alignment. The OSM also continually kicks the tyres.

Influence strategy falls squarely within the OSM's remit, with the Chief Influence Officer taking the associated 'integrator' role.

Constructing the Influence Scorecard

An organization's influence strategy describes how it expects to influence and be influenced in ways that are wholly necessary and sufficient for the successful execution of the overarching strategy. Its Influence Scorecard must therefore identify and measure the essential metrics associated with the way you've decided to go about influencing and being influenced.

Earlier in The Barcelona Principles section (pages 45–47) I alluded to the follow-up work underway to establish the 'validated metrics' to replace the discredited advertising value equivalence (AVE). The first draft of this work was presented at the AMEC PRSA PR Measurement Metrics Conference in London in November 2010.

The crux of the matter is that it makes no difference whether we're talking about PR, marketing, customer service or grounds maintenance; what is a valid metric to you may be an invalid one to me. Or, more precisely, just as it is for wider business performance management, the validity of an influence performance metric is entirely a function of your influence strategy and operations. However, as you've reached this point in this book, you already know that.

Of course, just because two different organizations happen to have different influence strategies does not mean they might not share the same influence performance metrics, and that's because it is the combination that's unique to the organization, not necessarily each metric.

In fact, perhaps one of my tweet responses to the conversation taking place around the October 2010 IPR (Institute of Public Relations) Summit on PR Measurement is the most concise I've given to date in explaining how I see things.[100]

> @richardbagnall Cheers. Reckon metrics as bespoke as strategy. 500+ 'standard' metrics. Curate handful most suited to strategy. #iprmeasure

It's amazing how a 140-character limit forces you to get to the point. We have many hundreds of 'standard' metrics related to PR activities, and I'm sure there are many hundreds more relating to marketing and other influence processes.

As you probably know, appropriate metrics are often called key performance indicators (KPIs).

Selecting your metrics

There are some great books that largely focus on various candidate metrics. Jim Sterne's *Social Media Metrics: How to Measure and Optimize your Marketing*

Measurement[101] is a very good read. As it was published in 2010 it does not, of course, follow our framework here, but deviation on that front aside it's a good resource for understanding how to design the metrics to suit your influence strategy in the domain of social media. I like his approach to chapter headings so I'm going to list them all here: getting focused; getting attention; getting respect; getting emotional; getting response; getting the message; getting results; getting buy-in; and getting ahead. And the best wake-up line in the book:

> The world of online marketing has been suffering from a delusion of precision and an expectation of exactitude.

Similarly, Katie Delahaye Paine's *Measure What Matters*,[102] published February 2011, will undoubtedly be excellent (I'm a fan). It looks at suitable metrics for social media, events, sponsorships, speaking engagements, thought leadership, relationships with your local community, what employees think, and reputational threats.

Marketing Metrics: The Definitive Guide to Measuring Marketing Performance[103] does what it says on the cover, and Kaplan and Norton's *Balanced Scorecard*,[104] as you'd expect, delivers an excellent overview of selecting the right measures and setting targets in general.

If you're stuck for ideas then you can always search online for inspiration from people who have previously approached similar problems. It was doing just this that I stumbled across the KPI Library,[105] SmartKPIs[106] and KPI Portal[107] websites for example, and the Ascendant Strategy Management Group has a nascent forum on all aspects of the Balanced Scorecard.[108] The Palladium Group hosts its by-application Execution Premium Community[109] (XPC) for those professionals dedicated to strategic alignment and execution.

As we've seen, entire books can be written on finding the right metrics for the right situations, and we cannot hope to live up to that level of detail here. As this influence framework is unprecedented, perhaps you'll join me in collating the first portfolio of influence KPIs at this book's accompanying website. I will, however, share with you my golden rules for metric selection:

- Only employ metrics that directly and obviously guide behaviour and performance as required by strategic objectives
- Metrics need each other – no metric can achieve what's needed alone
- Metrics must complement not compete
- Just because something is easy to measure, or is already measured, does not qualify it as a good metric
- When you have a choice of two equally appropriate metrics, select the most readily understood
- Never employ fewer or more metrics than will suffice
- Metrics with unneeded side effects aren't quite right – redesign them; or, a metric that can be gamed demands a complementary metric to ensure that it isn't.

The AMEC grid

Table 7.4 is a representation of the grid developed by AMEC and PRSA supported by the CIPR and PRCA following the Barcelona Conference in 2010.[110] The original idea was to populate each of the white grid squares with validated metrics, but given that we assert here that 'valid' is entirely contingent on one's strategy, I regard the output of this work to be the empty grid itself – go forth and fill it in, within the boundaries of the Influence Scorecard of course.

At the time of writing, the AMEC team appears intent on providing example metrics in each grid square, which is most welcome as long as those

Table 7.4: The AMEC grid

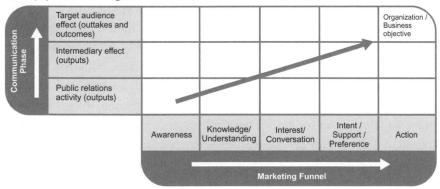

who want to integrate this work into their public relations activity consider the example metrics to be just that: candidates rather than prescriptions. KPIs should fit the strategy, not the other way around. The AMEC work proposes listing metrics for each 'key area of communication', which I understand to include brand / product marketing, reputation building, issues advocacy / support, employee engagement, investor relations, and crisis/ issues management.

The writing of this book predates the London Measurement Conference, so I can't describe the corresponding debate and agreement, but a quick hop to AMEC's website[III] will get you up to speed.

The diagonal arrow of the AMEC grid can be read as representing the heart of the matter here. Metrics towards the bottom left are incredibly easy to develop. The possibilities are abundant; they are easily quantified, but unfortunately they're not closely related to the organizational objective. You should expect to see such relatively useless metrics (in terms of having, or rather not having, proven cause-and-effect linkage to strategic objectives) as 'eyeballs' or impressions towards this end. Seriously, when did we last quantify success in the real world by the number of people who walked *past* our shop – but on the basis that they did at least see our sign?

The metrics towards the arrowhead, in the top right grid squares, are considerably more difficult to define, are more likely to require tailoring to marry appropriately to the strategic objectives, and will probably be harder to quantify – at least to quantify with sufficient frequency. Yet, of course, they hold greater potential in describing organizational performance.

When seeking the appropriate KPIs to measure the degree of success with which your organization is executing its influence strategy, it's worth keeping this spectrum in mind, gravitating towards the top right without hobbling yourself. In fact you might recognize that we've already discussed this – the act of tracing influence is most definitely driving towards that arrowhead.

Given that this grid is under development literally as I write, it seemed the obvious example to choose. But this same story of finding the most appropriate KPIs plays out for every aspect of influence, not just public relations. Indeed, it plays out for every aspect of business performance.

The grid is AMEC's first attempt at finding an alternative to AVE and is bound to morph in coming years as practice illuminates its strengths and weaknesses. I obviously believe it will be a far more useful device if employed within our influence framework as a way to help to divine the right metrics. And indeed, thinking on that for a moment reminds me of Kaplan and Norton's customer perspective consisting of the four steps – select, acquire, retain, and grow customers. Organizational success is no longer defined sale by sale but rather by the development of long-term, profitable relationships with targeted customers. Perhaps, then, the application of the marketing funnel to the horizontal access may turn out to be a weakness in its ability to help to identify appropriate metrics if 'action' is translated simply in terms of ringing up the cash register. Will select, acquire, retain, and grow make for a more useful x-axis?

Budgeting

Given the inspiration for the Influence Scorecard, and given the fact that it is the Six Influence Flows manifest in the Balanced Scorecard, its construction by definition enables us to prioritize investments in influence-related human, information and organization capital. This is a process that lives and breathes within organizations that use the Balanced Scorecard. It doesn't quite kill the budget fight, because the tension isn't fuelled by ego or who-shouts-loudest or who-knows-who but by transparent rationale. Certainly, heads will continue to champion their corner, but their weapons can only be strategy development, innovation and communication. No more lazy reliance on small tweaks to last year's budget, but a fresh, zero-based budgeting approach that aspires to meet the coming year's unique challenges and opportunities.

ROI

I dislike any attempt to hijack the term ROI. Accountants know what ROI means, and they can only view any softening or redirection or substitution of its meaning by marketers trying to validate their investment plans as smoke and mirrors. You won't find anything in this book about a 'return on influence' for example – oh, except just there of course.

For one rather entertaining perspective on ROI, in the domain of social media, take a few minutes to listen to David Meerman Scott 'rant'.[112] At first you might think David is advocating the abandonment of any calculation of the worth of social media, but he's not. He's just saying that MBA courses are preaching the wrong approach: an approach more akin to the attitude to ROI that is integral to integrated marketing communications, as we'll tease out later. David believes that business leaders have been hiding behind the ROI argument out of fear of social media. From conversations with him, I know he considers social media to be a strategic imperative, an imperative that is given complete validity by the Influence Scorecard as and when demanded by each organization's influence strategy.

I thank my colleague Gabbi Cahane for alerting me to this apt H.L. Mencken quote: 'For every complex problem there is an answer that is clear, simple, and wrong.' And as much as I'd dearly love to present a simple answer to ROI, I'm afraid the Influence Scorecard is as close as we're going to get. The temptation to develop a simpler framework is teasing, but the omission of any step, nuance or reliance only serves to break rather than simplify the model.

This reminds me of a pet hate – the slide in the too typical introduction-to-social-media presentation that preaches something like: 'Remember, we do social media for one reason – to sell.' Not only does the presenter not understand how unsuited the verb 'to do' is in this context (you might 'do' advertising, but in my opinion you don't 'do' conversation), but also they obviously struggle to couch social media in a suitable strategic framework as we do here.

John Bell's 'CMO's dilemma' referred to the CMO's struggle with social media ROI and his sentiment is echoed in *Twitter, Twitter, Little Stars*, a *Business Week* article, July 2010.[113] Describing the role of the social media officer as possibly the 'zaniest human resources innovation in memory', the article plants tongue firmly in cheek in outlining the two-step process that companies go through in this regard:

> First, they scramble to hire social media officers. Second, they figure out what it is, exactly, that social media officers do.

And then this damning indictment:

> Much of the justification for the corporate spending [in social media], however, is anecdotal. As company chiefs find themselves chasing

another new, new thing in the digital world, they are doing so as much on faith and emotion as on metrics and case history.

Social media, it seems, has well and truly joined the role call of marketing and PR-related activities for which ROI calculation remains stubbornly illusive.

Pat LaPointe, Managing Partner of MarketingNPV, maintains a blog titled *Marketing Measurement Today*.[114] It's a worthwhile read – so take a look around if you haven't yet come across it. LaPointe and I have never met or spoken, so it's entirely coincidental that as I'm writing this section, he has posted: 'Measurement problems? Check your credibility chain.'[115] In this post he reminds readers that metrics must be aligned to the needs of the business, comprehensive and objective, and lead to accountability. Our viewpoints have much in common but I feel that LaPointe's approach to ROI, while endeavouring to be more thorough than you'll find in most organizations that feign such attempts, errs in being too simplistic.

His July 2009 post, 'Twittering away time and money',[116] opens with:

> One of the most common questions I'm getting these days is 'How should I measure the value of all the social marketing things we're doing like Twitter, Linked-in, Facebook, etc.?'
>
> My answer: WHY are you doing them in the first place? If you can't answer that, you're wasting your time and the company's money.

LaPointe then lays out a six-step framework for thinking about social measurement, starting with:

> Fill in the blanks: 'Adding or swapping-in social media initiatives will impact _____ by _____ extent over _____ timeframe. And when that happens, the added value for the business will be $_____, which will give me an ROI of _____.'
> This forms your hypotheses about what you might achieve, and why the rest of the business should care.

The ensuing five steps involve sensitivity analysis, flexing the assumptions to find the most sensitive variables, conducting small-scale experiments to learn more about these variables, and reiterating until you have a model that seems to work. He asserts that the drivers of success become apparent, and these form your key metrics.

If LaPointe can achieve in six-steps, and in one blog post, what has taken me the best part of a book, then I'm in trouble. I don't think polarizing the situation with a closed question like 'Does it work?' helps. I have no doubt that the process LaPointe proposes has value, if not just prompting organizations to think about what they're doing in a wider organizational context, but here's my beef.

The primary problem is once again the one that David Meerman Scott rants about. Not every aspect of social marketing can be quantified as having a return in hard cash, and the fact that one aspect might lend itself to this analysis doesn't mean that it's more suited to helping the organization to achieve its ends than other aspects that can't. Try to fill in those blanks above for the idea of starting a CEO blog, or a Facebook campaign, or an investment in social Web analytics, or a store redesign, or executing a new call centre strategy. And if you can't answer these points singly, how might an answer be derived from considering a social media campaign in its entirety? I mean, really, where do you start?

LaPointe is on the money, if you'll forgive the pun, in asking: 'WHY are you doing them in the first place?', but his 'fill in the blanks' step assumes that only answers for which you have any chance of estimating a number after the dollar sign can be proffered. Having stressed organizational alignment, it seems that it can only be alignment in the financial perspective, not the intangibles in the learning and growth perspective that have strategic linkage to the operations, and then customer perspectives.

I'm also uncomfortable effectively coming up with something constituting a social media initiative and then testing it. I'd rather the 'something' emerged from diligent left- and right-brained deliberations following the cascade of mission > values > vision > strategy > strategy mapping > scorecard.

There is another problem, one relating to the small-scale experiments. Having been involved in my fair share of operations modelling and simulation over the years, I'd advise caution in linearly extrapolating any results from small-scale experiments in situations where scale may be a non-linear factor. Doing so may well significantly overestimate the outcome and lead to returns that are considerably lower than expected, or significantly underestimate the potential and thereby kill ideas that may otherwise have proved productive. But this isn't the forum to explain why, particularly as this isn't my primary objection here.

In the face of chaos

A section on facing chaos would have been trickier to pen in 2007. Apart from the sector specific 'dot.bomb' in 2001, business life had been in a fairly steady state for a decade and a half. No one can argue now, however, that an acid test for any strategic framework must be its ability to help leaders to face up to chaotic conditions (no one, that is, until the next generation is smiling comfortably a decade or so into the next supposed end of boom and bust).

If this is a subject that interests you, I recommend *Chaotics: The Business of Managing and Marketing in the Age of Turbulence*[117] by Philip Kotler and John Caslione. This is how they see the too-typical response when things get stormy:

> When it comes time to make cuts, marketing always seems to get the first swipe, and new product development the second. This is always a mistake because it destroys market share and innovation. . . . When you cut marketing, you are leaving room for your competitors to get their message out in the forefront and to gain greater market share as yours slips away.

The authors also discuss a natural tendency to focus on the here-and-now transactional customers when times get tight. But such customers are fickle, and always looking for the best deal. The appropriate strategy, they stress, is to continue investing in the relational customers, the ones looking for a relationship with a trusted brand – looking for expertise over price.

Let's take a quick look at how the Influence Scorecard helps organizations in tough, unpredictable times. But, first, a summary of how Kotler and Caslione view the typical situation today in a chapter dedicated to designing marketing systems for resilience:

> Today, the typical company operates a marketing system that has
> emerged from years of trial and error. It has developed policies, strate-
> gies, and tactics for using marketing research, pricing, the sales force,
> advertising, promotions, trade shows, and other marketing tools. These
> practices are likely to persist because they deliver a feeling of safety and
> predictability. They worked in the past and are assumed to work in the
> future.

I would go further. Today too many companies operate marketing and
public relations as cost centres rather than strategically critical components
of their wider influence strategy, a point also made in support of the integrated marketing communications approach by Schultz and Schultz in their
book *IMC – The Next Generation.*[118] The emphasis is on communicating out,
not on sensitizing the organization to the zeitgeist. The emphasis is on operational excellence, not strategic excellence, and responsive adaptation is all but
impossible when operational excellence has to date been adjudged by, and is
reliant upon, steady-state conditions.

The authors propose an eight-phase chaotics implementation cycle:

1. Identify sources of turbulence and chaos
2. Identify management's wrong responses to turbulence
3. Establish early-warning systems
4. Construct key scenarios and strategies
5. Prioritize key scenarios and select a strategy
6. Implement chaotics strategic management behaviours
7. Implement chaotics strategic marketing behaviours
8. Achieve business enterprise sustainability.

Number 2 was a bit of a surprise for me, but I imagine, with hindsight, that
the best way to know wrong behaviour when you need to think fast is to have
identified wrong behaviours in advance. I like it.

Their number 3 is where the Influence Scorecard begins to step up to the
challenge. Half of that is courtesy of Kaplan and Norton of course, and
the Balanced Scorecard's emphasis on leading indicators. If you're driving
into a storm looking in the rear view mirror, you're not going to see the storm

as early as you otherwise would. Chaotic conditions demand *flexibility*, the ability to adjust operations as required to continue to execute the strategy optimally, and *adaptability*, the ability to recognize when the current strategy has lost its relevance and new a strategy is demanded. Flexibility is informed by single-loop learning, and adaptability by double-loop learning.

The other half relates to the integration of all things influence. With your cohesive and coherent enterprise-wide influence operations sensitized to the 3rd flow (our stakeholders' influence with us) from all stakeholders, more needles have the potential to start twitching, to be systematically visible and more noticeably visible when twitching together. To deny this is to disregard a vital sense or two, or to deny their heightening in holistic combination.

For clarity, it's not unusual for an organization to have a systematic approach to setting, measuring and responding to KPIs today, but the Influence Scorecard demands a greater degree of synchrony and unification of those KPIs relating to all Six Influence Flows with all stakeholders. It recognizes that these KPIs share a certain affinity and combinatory potential that sets them apart from non-influence related KPIs.

Kotler and Caslione assert that business leaders must create organizations that are responsive, robust and resilient; they define 'responsive' simply as the quality of being able to react quickly to external stimuli. Speed of response is partly a function of the speed with which the signals are detected, connected, cross-referenced, collated, filtered and interpreted (3rd flow). Responsiveness also encompasses the speed with which the outbound influence can be tweaked to represent, as required by the influence strategy, the changes wrought inside the organization in response to external conditions (1st flow – our influence with our stakeholders).

The Influence Scorecard also assists in the achievement of steps 6 and 7 above. Obviously the authors did not approach their book with our new framework in mind, so they have chosen to view the organization in terms of marketing (step 7) and everything else (step 6). It would be interesting to restructure the book's content according to those aspects of organizations relating to influence and everything else, but for now suffice it to say that the Influence Scorecard helps to gear the organization to the influence-related needs identified in both these steps in the chaotics implementation cycle.

I conclude that the Influence Scorecard is a powerful approach to navigating chaos.

Influence capability maturity model

The Software Engineering Institute maintains the Capability Maturity Model – a model for improving software development processes pioneered via the collection of actual field data to help to determine best practice. The Influence Scorecard might spawn the development of an influence capability maturity model for the improvement of influence processes. Perhaps this might build on the research begun in *The Future for Marketing Capability* report by the CIM and Accenture.[119]

Another scorecard

Forrester Research proposed a 'balanced marketing scorecard' in its July 2010 report, *The ROI of Social Media Marketing* (reproduced with permission). (I won't belabour the differences between marketing and PR again.) The motivation for the report is one I share whole-heartedly as you'll know by now; it refers to the desire to determine ROI but that 'many benefits delivered by social media are not easily measured in dollars and cents'.

The report doesn't reference the work we started here in 2009 but takes quite a different stance entirely. It refers to Kaplan and Norton's augmentation of the financial perspective with the three non-financial perspectives – or 'indirectly financial' in the words of the report – and then presents a way forward for social media:

> Because social media delivers a broad range of advantages to marketers, a similar approach [to the Balanced Scorecard] is necessary to fully capture the value delivered by social media programs and tools. A balanced social media marketing scorecard will consider and monitor effects across four perspectives that balance the short term and long term and the directly financial with indirectly financial outcomes.

It prescribes digital, brand and risk management perspectives in addition to the financial perspective. The digital perspective is qualified by the question: 'Has the company enhanced its owned and earned digital assets?'; the brand perspective by: 'Have consumer attitudes about the brand improved?'; and the risk management perspective by: 'Is the organization better prepared to note and respond to attacks or problems that affect reputation?'

I think this is the wrong way to go. First, it appears to ignore the value of social media dialogue with other stakeholders beyond consumers, but that's a small point compared to my main criticism.

The Balanced Scorecard is anchored in the mission, values and vision of the organization, with the accompanying strategy maps clearly portraying the causes and effects. There is no other anchor. It's not that Kaplan and Norton alighted on some non-financial perspectives in isolation, but that they identified universal leading-indicator perspectives pertaining to what the organization was striving to achieve.

Despite the claim, the Forrester scorecard is not 'a similar approach'. Similarity is not achieved by picking some non-financial perspectives to go alongside the financial perspective any time you have an aspect of business that doesn't quite lend itself to hard currency. That's like saying a dining chair and a horse are similar because they both have four legs and you sit on them. Similarity, as indeed we see in other BPM approaches, comes from establishing an unremitting, rational cascade of the organization's objectives to the day-to-day reality, with single-loop and double-loop learning.

I'd go further. In my view, this proposal from Forrester is precisely in the danger zone we highlighted earlier when we referred to the need for 'initiative killing' to achieve and maintain alignment.

On the face of it, who is going to argue at the coalface (or indeed around the board table of companies without rigorous BPM) with maxims relating to enhancing digital assets, or improving consumer attitudes, or being better prepared to respond to reputational risks? No one. The report certainly makes some interesting points and asks some excellent questions, and we must continue to challenge established thinking and explore new frameworks, but not, I'd argue, under the auspices of an unmoored scorecard.

Forrester's balanced marketing scorecard is a distraction as far as we are concerned here. Similar or not, we don't need a *similar* approach; we need the *same* approach. The Influence Scorecard works *into* the Balanced Scorecard, not separately from it. It's the very integration with the tried and tested Balanced Scorecard that grants us the empirical evidence to say that all aligned influence activities will – if well executed with the appropriate metrics to adjudge success – deliver the ROI we so desperately need.

The Influence Scorecard and integrated marketing communications

At the end of the first chapter ('Where We Are Today'), I introduced integrated marketing communications (IMC) as the vision that describes how marketing and PR and the rest of the organization are supposed to come together. I also referred to my intention to compare our influence framework with the 2003 book by Schultz and Schultz, *IMC – The Next Generation: Five Steps for Delivering Value and Measuring Returns using Marketing Communications.*[120] And here we are.

I'll repeat the definition of IMC used in their book:

> Integrated marketing communication is a strategic business process used to plan, develop, create, and evaluate coordinated, measurable, persuasive brand communication programs over time, with consumers, customers, prospects, and other targeted, relevant external and internal audiences.

The authors' five-step process is:

1. Identifying customers and prospects
2. Estimating the value of customers and prospects
3. Planning communication messages and incentives
4. Estimating return on customer investment (ROCI)
5. Postprogram [sic] analysis and future planning.

The authors assert that IMC lifts 'marcom' activities from the tactical role to strategic management tool, and they repeatedly make the claim that the five-step process allows for clear-cut investment decisions to be made and financial returns to be calculated. Needless to say, if I thought that this was playing out repeatedly in reality, I wouldn't have drafted in the empirically proven Balanced Scorecard here.

On the face of it, the IMC approach appears to share something in common with our influence framework, and we need to take a look at this in a little more detail before returning to the ROI (or ROCI) question. We seem to share an emphasis on the customer. The Balanced Scorecard obviously has the customer perspective and the Schultz IMC approach adheres ardently to customer-centricity.

> Our view is simple but clear: the organization must focus on its end-user customers and consumers. Those are the only people or groups that can provide income to the firm. Customer-generated income flows enable the company to provide employee benefits; reward shareholders for their investment and risk; and provide society with the benefits a well-run, socially responsible organization can generate.

Our influence framework obviously has a similarly high regard for customers, at least when the organization's mission – as conveyed by the quote above – has a for-profit motivation. Indeed, earlier I referred to customers as the most powerful engines of organizational success. But perhaps customer-centricity as articulated in *IMC – The Next Generation* doesn't do the best job of centring the business. Sure, it's more current and more intuitive than the inward-focused organization-centric emphases of the past but, despite the inclusion of other stakeholders in the definition of IMC, it still feels to me like an oversimplification. For example, if an organization pays too much attention to customers' apparent needs in detriment to the attention it pays to working with environmental lobbyists and addressing their concerns, it risks a quick and severe backlash from those very customers it was trying so hard to keep happy. Similarly, I'm a customer of more than one organization for the very reason that they strive to put the environment's needs ahead of mine and I can afford the occasionally greater cost and perhaps slightly inferior product.

If you're giving the customer what she wants, but she then finds that your supply chain involves so-called sweatshops in lesser-developed parts of the world, then . . . well, we've seen how that goes around. If, in your customer-centric world, you stretch the goodwill of your staff or partners just that little bit too much, then when it snaps it's those precious customers – and your business – who are going to suffer. And often a snapping isn't required, just a gentle disgruntlement.

The original Balanced Scorecard was criticized for its emphasis of the customer above other stakeholders, and Kaplan and Norton moderated it accordingly as we've discussed – customers remain boldly front and centre with a whole perspective dedicated to them, but the Balanced Scorecard and strategy maps do not allow for an imbalance when your strategy is mapped and your metrics are selected.

Our framework demands an appropriate balance of the Six Influence Flows with all stakeholders. Short-term organizational success may be achieved when optimizing just one facet of business, and such one-hit or one-time wonders will always catch the eye, but long-term success can only be assured by optimizing the appropriate balance that best executes your strategy.

Rather than seeing the customer as a maypole around which the organization dances, our framework views the customer more like a ball-bearing in the middle of a butler's tray that can only be kept centred in high winds and along bumpy roads by continuous deft adjustments to the tray's attitude. This analogy isn't perfect, however, as achieving the optimal strategic balance is considerably more difficult.

Perhaps that ball-bearing isn't the customer after all, but simply represents the balance every organization must strive to achieve and maintain, via strategic alignment with single- and double-loop learning, in order to maximize delivery against objectives.

Perhaps putting the customer first requires that one does not? Or, in other words, perhaps long-term customer loyalty is best achieved when the customer witnesses personally the balance you work hard to attain, or simply the consistently delightful fruits of those labours.

If your organization's strategy recognizes the criticality of all types of stakeholders with a balancing of the resources invested in influence flows as unique as the strategy, why would you adopt a framework, IMC, which confesses a disconnected and untailored priority?

Let's return to complexity. The customer-centricity of IMC implies that our approach to marketing communications will be guided primarily by the marketing communications between the organization and its customers. Yet outcomes such as reputation, trust and significance crystallize from influence flows, and the influence flows between an organization and a customer and its other stakeholders are not only affected by marketing and public relations activities, but also by other stakeholder touch-point activities that aren't categorized as marketing or communications. Moreover, influence flows between the organization and one stakeholder group don't exist in isolation from the influence flows with other stakeholder groups; they can and do jumble. It's a complex system. I've said it before – it's all in the mix.

Schultz and Schultz most definitely agree that this goes wider than marketing and PR:

> While here we discuss the management of income flows as the primary task of marketing and communication people, in truth, it is the responsibility of the entire firm, all employees, all functional groups, all elements to develop, cultivate, and maintain those customer income flows over time.

It seems, then, that everyone has a hand in 'income flows', yet the authors claim return on customer investment (ROCI) as marcom's own. So let's focus on this financial calculation.

> If they are to be strategic . . . marketing and communication must prove their worth in terms of demonstrable returns to the organization. This is where the IMC approach succeeds and traditional marketing initiatives – even the much-touted CRM – fail. By providing demonstrable returns, we mean that IMC must go much further than traditional communication goals such as building brand awareness or recognition. It must achieve management's financial goals, too.

This relentless focus on 'income flows' will undoubtedly delight Mike Smock and those who, like Mike, considered the American Marketing Association's new definition of marketing to fall short in this regard, as you may recall from earlier (see 'Marketing' on page 6). The authors go to some lengths to outline their recommendations for assessing the likely value of customers and prospects, in the short term (business-building) and long term (brand-building), and thereby arrive at an estimate of ROCI. In the short term:

> . . . a postcommunication [sic] measurement can be made to determine the change in income flow that resulted from that investment, allowing the firm to close the loop on its marketing and communication investments.

If you work in a large, mature, predictable market with competitors not wishing to disrupt the status quo, and if you're happy to ignore the roles other processes play, it might just be something you'd like to explore. Similarly, if you operate in a relatively simple and quiet market in which you have the freedom to change just one aspect of your operations at a time, you may try a new ad campaign. I admit I have no experience of either. Ultimately, the authors highlight some of the non-trivial challenges that most practitioners will experience in trying to follow this approach, and it seems that, in the absence of anything better, they recommend that you get on with it.

But almost every marketing and PR practitioner I've ever spoken with on this matter – some fluent in the IMC approach and some not – accept that attributing incremental 'income flow' to a particular marketing or PR tactic or set of tactics is nigh impossible more often than not. They know that there are too many factors to control, producing too much noise. They don't articulate it as such, but they know it's a complex system.

Significantly, whereas we discuss the *customer perspective* as a leading indicator here – an indicator of today's business performance that helps management to get a handle on the numbers that will likely drop out in future quarters in the financial perspective – *marketing communications* is described as having a 'lagged effect' in *IMC – The Next Generation*. In this context, 'lagged effect' refers to the delay in a customer seeing or hearing a communication and acting on it. Of course we're all looking at the same coin, but from different sides. We're focused here on strategically-aligned non-financial metrics that belie the degree to which we're living up to our own plans to do the right things, and practitioners following the IMC path are trying to do things right by the CFO and other dollar-driven (rather than strategy-driven) members of the management team.

I feel an affinity with Schultz and Schultz, although we have never met. We're trying to address the same problems, and while I have dedicated most of this section to explaining the differences between the influence framework and IMC, and justifying those differences in favour of the influence framework of course, I've discovered some interesting common viewpoints in the course of researching this chapter.

For example, *IMC – The Next Generation* concludes with a section on future directions in which the authors argue for a need to move to a behavioural approach to measurement and evaluation focused on what people do rather than on how they feel following marketing communication. This is a component of our tracing influence, and the intervening years of technological revolution have made this increasingly possible.

And, most excitingly, in the same section on future directions, the authors write:

> In order to tell senior management exactly what will come back if money is invested in certain ways, marketers must move from measuring what happened in the past to what might happen in the future.

If that's not the strongest endorsement for the Balanced Scorecard / Influence Scorecard and its lead indicators, I don't know what is. We don't feel compelled to translate every non-financial metric into dollars, pounds and euros, but the deterministic nature of the metrics is built-in by design. Perhaps, then, our influence framework is the future direction that the Schultzes anticipated?

I'll conclude this section by reworking the earlier quote from *IMC – The Next Generation*: 'If they are to be strategic . . . marketing and communication must prove their worth in terms of demonstrable returns to the organization.' This is how I would put it: If marketing and communication are to prove their worth to the organization, they must be measured continuously for alignment with the organization's influence strategy, which in turn must be wholly aligned with the overarching strategy.

Summary

- The Influence Scorecard is the act of setting measures, targets and reporting – the subset or view of the Balanced Scorecard containing all the influence-related KPIs stripped of functional silo
- The Influence Scorecard is the philosophy and management approach
- It is both part of, and an augmentation to, the Balanced Scorecard (or similar BPM approach). It can only thrive in organizations already practising business performance management effectively
- The Chief Influence Officer and team will form the organization's specific influence objectives from the organization's mission, values and vision
- Influence objectives may be set by organizational objective by stakeholder
- A SBU may be defined as being an entity with one universal set of influence objectives
- Influence objectives may be determined by mapping the 'journey' of each stakeholder type and exploring the influence touch points of such a journey
- The influence strategy describes how an organization expects to influence and be influenced in ways that are wholly necessary and sufficient to the achievement of the influence objectives and successful execution of the overarching strategy
- Only an organization-wide strategic approach that (a) puts influence at the centre of organizational strategy, (b) enables single- and double-loop learning, and (c) applies a Balanced Scorecard type approach, will produce the kind of results the board and influence professionals need and all stakeholders want
- Dealing with intangible assets in a professional manner is difficult to the point of impossibility without this kind of approach
- The Chief Influence Officer takes the 'integrator' role with the OSM.
- Metric selection is a critical task
- The Influence Scorecard doesn't quite kill the budget fight, because the tension isn't fuelled by ego or who-shouts-loudest or who-knows-who but by transparent rationale
- There is no shorter route to doing the right things, to achieving the strategy and securing ROI, than the Influence Scorecard.

- The Influence Scorecard is a powerful approach to navigating chaotic market conditions
- If marketing and communication are to prove their worth to the organization, they must be measured continuously for alignment with the organization's influence strategy, which in turn must be wholly aligned with the overarching strategy.

That was a pretty intense chapter. Let's lift ourselves up from the nuances of objectives, strategy, metrics, budgeting and ROI, and take a look at some of the big trends surrounding our influence professionals.

8

In this chapter we explore some of the big trends every influence professional should understand: mobile and other things, privacy and influence flow sharing, buyer marketing and Web 3.0.

Mobile and other things

We have a framework with Six Influence Flows, but what are these flows exactly? From an analogue communications perspective the flows are information exchange processed by human minds, and from a digital perspective the flows are data moving between things on the network which are easily processed and archived by information technologies for indexing, searching and statistical analysis, and may also, ultimately, form information processed by human minds.

Until the turn of the century the Internet was generally considered to be a network of computers, where computers could be the servers operated by large organizations and hosts, massive desktop things in our homes and offices, and portable things called laptops. That changed with the widespread adoption of the smartphone, a phone that by definition has data connectivity capabilities and usually some sort of powerful operating system and capable Web browser. And if we're talking époques, then the history of the smartphone may now be considered to consist of the pre-iPhone and post-iPhone (2007) eras, given the step change in our expectations of a smartphone following the iPhone launch.

The data constituting the digital element of influence flows is sent and received by servers, desktop computers, laptops, mobiles and, as we shall see, other things. But let's dwell for a moment on the phone.

Phones are the most personal of consumer electronic devices. They rank with keys and money when going out. They become an extension of their owner and their loss is mourned, literally.

Smartphones are the most personal of all digital devices. They are so advanced over the early mobile telephones that the word 'phone' persists in the name only for atavistic reasons. A smartphone is an address book, diary, digital messenger, Web browser, games machine, music player, video player, navigator, video and stills camera . . . and, of course, a phone. It keeps you connected with those far away, and disengaged from strangers nearby.

Approximately the first billion people linked to the Internet via the traditional computing devices: the desktop and laptop. The rest of the world's population has accessed or will access the Internet for the first time via phones.

Therefore, when a marketer wants to make a connection, what better platform than the one considered the most personal and emotional? It is invariably with its owner who always knows where it is.

Without listing every set of mobile marketing tactics it appears, then, to be the domain in which permission marketing is most critical. Increased emotional attachment to the device increases the emotional interaction with, and attachment to, the 'stuff' the phone's owner wants to put on it, and quite possibly the emotional reaction to 'stuff' he or she does not.

And this is where we meet the fuzzy lines between giving (a) specific permission (phone owner: 'dear Nikon, do keep me posted about Nikon'), (b) general permission (phone owner: 'dear service provider, I'm interested in photography') and (c) behavioural targeting (service provider: 'Hi, we're tracking what you've been doing and we think you're interested in photography'). We return to this topic in the 'Privacy' section below.

The most interesting developments in mobile marketing in recent times must be Google's acquisition of AdMob in November 2009, closely followed by Apple's acquisition of Quattro Wireless in January 2010. At the time of writing, the market is looking closely at the remaining independent mobile advertising and technology companies.

Other mobile marketing developments to keep abreast of include augmented reality and other location-based innovations (particularly the fight for 'check-in' between, for example, FourSquare, Gowalla, Facebook Places, Twitter Places and others), mobile social relationship management, the integration of paid and earned media, in-game advertising, mobile digital content streaming, mobile search advertising, and mobile payment services.

And if the phone/personal digital 'thing' isn't enough to keep influence professionals busily occupied, there are others. There is, for example, the Internet of Things, which refers to a network of objects not historically connected. We can consider four kinds of objects: the device containing electronics in order to fulfil its primary function (e.g. washing machines, air conditioning units and cars); the electrical device traditionally absent of sophisticated electronics (e.g. lighting, electric heaters, and power distribution); non-electrical objects (e.g. food and drink packages, clothes, and animals); and environmental sensors measuring variables (e.g. temperature, noise and moisture).

Just in case you were wondering how non-electrical items join the Internet if they have no electrical power, I'm referring here to something called radio frequency identification (RFID), which we discussed briefly in the business context part of the Introduction (see page xxi). This technology is manifest with small tags that are physically attached to the item in question and can be active (by battery), but are now more often passive (no battery). The tags hold digital information about the item and can be read remotely as the item arrives at the warehouse, for example, or as a cow is milked, or as a traveller uses her payment card on public transport, or her passport going through passport control, or as a book is checked in and out of a library.

I have seen estimates for the total number of items connected to the Internet of Things that vary from 16 billion in 2020 to more than 30 times that number. Either way, the 'things' will outnumber the approximately 7 billion people on the planet by some margin.

In his 1999 book, *Business @ The Speed of Thought*,[121] Bill Gates refers to the organizational IT infrastructure as the digital nervous system analogous to the biological autonomic nervous system. The Internet of Things marks the point at which the Internet becomes the biological autonomic nervous system of the planet, and the influence professional will be a student of the impulses (data) conveyed along these nerves where they constitute influence flows. Perhaps the 1st flow (our influence with our stakeholders) is the organization's motor nerve and the 3rd flow (our stakeholders' influence with us) is its sensory nerve, but I'm always cautious of overextending analogies so I'll stop there. Particularly as I'm no student of biology.

I organized the first day-long conference on the Internet of Things in the UK, November 2010 – Internetome. The Internetome was defined as the manifestations of the Internet of Things and I polemically mooted that the Internetome itself might become an organizational stakeholder of sorts. If emergent behaviours stem from 2 billion humans, as we discussed earlier, we can expect something similar from the 'real world' interacting with tens of billions of things.

New opportunities

The Internet of Things transforms, or at least has major ramifications for, almost every sector and discipline I can think of. Our focus in this book is on the Six Influence Flows, the new influence professional and the Influence Scorecard management approach, so while the influence professional will work closely with the Internet of Things, now is not the time to explore how it transforms product and service development and marketing opportunities more broadly. However, I will leave you with some teaser questions that apply right here right now. This particular set of questions pivots around the fact that you no longer need to 'lose touch' with your products. You can 'talk' to them, and they can 'talk' back.

- Does Sony sell TVs, or a home entertainment service?
- Does Fiat sell cars, or a transportation service?
- Does Bosch sell dishwashers, or a dishwashing service?
- How might preventative maintenance be designed and marketed?
- How is the concept of a warranty transformed?
- How might such a redesign of the proposition lay new foundations for a lifetime relationship with the customer?
- How might the Internet of Things impact the visibility of your organization's impact on the environment?

We will also address related issues in the next section.

Privacy, data ownership and sharing

We shall later define the skills and knowledge required of an influence profes-sional and the Chief Influence Officer. Some of those skills will entail devel-oping a command of existing facets of the influence processes, such as search engine marketing or research methodology for example, and some of those skills will be unique to what it means to be an influence professional. I con-sider a solid grasp of privacy and influence flow sharing to be central to the role definition. (Actually, privacy falls in both camps; there is existing privacy policy and there is the new privacy policy, as we'll now see.)

Who owns the data?

There's money in them thar flows.

The focus in this brief section is the ownership of that data and informa-tion. I say brief because in my mind the situation is clear-cut, at least from my grasp of the expected societal norms of liberal democracies, or, perhaps more accurately, the norms I'd prefer to live with.

That's not to say, however, that my preference is how things will turn out, far from it; nor is it ignoring the fact that norms can change. But this book isn't the place for an in-depth social philosophy discourse. It is worth pointing out that I do detect contradictory expectations on this topic however, most strongly in the USA, as I describe below.

This is how I see it.

I consider the data and information I create directly or indirectly through my use of products and services to be private and mine by default. I may choose to make any part of it accessible to specified others and maintain my ownership, or relinquish some ownership rights, or all rights.

Should I consider entering a contract with the purchase of a product or service that entails some variation to this default – perhaps simply because delivery of the product or service is meaningless without such variation – the nature of this variation must be made explicitly clear to me in plain language, and it is then my choice whether or not to agree to those terms, which may entail my negotiating different terms or choosing not to buy that specific product or service.

That's my take. What's yours?

For the sake of a quick sanity check I frequently run this way of looking at it by individuals who are not entrenched in this sort of thing for a living. If you are entrenched, try looking at it with fresh eyes or indeed ask someone with fresh eyes to tell you how they see it. On chatting it through casually, I have not met one individual who objected. Not one. Rather, they nod as if that's how the world spins and the birds sing in the morning.

The tension I feel most strongly in the USA relates to the uncertainty regarding who has precedence in these relationships. On the one hand I see US citizens vehemently defending civil liberties, particularly as framed by the Constitution, and on the other hand I see a more rampant capitalism that lends the body corporate more leeway than they might enjoy in Europe. (I'm afraid my appreciation of the situation in other parts of the world is poor.) Should the US corporate take precedent in this regard the default will be that this data belongs to the supplier of the product or service rather than the consumer or citizen.

Charles Braithwaite, a commercial lawyer, intellectual property expert and partner at the London-based Collyer Bristow firm of solicitors, is quoted in the following extract of a 2010 article in *Engineering & Technology* magazine article forebodingly entitled *Who Owns You?*[122]

> Much of the unease surrounding Internet privacy may come down to nothing more than transatlantic differences of habit. European legislation protects our data against misuse, but as Braithwaite points out, in the US, the base of global Internet giants, 'similar legislation is thin on the ground. In Europe data protection is granted even after the consumer has passed on the data, whereas in the US there still seems to be an understanding by companies that once they have the information they can do largely what they want with it.'

Nor is the situation in Europe far from clear cut. What if one looks at retail as a service, for example? Tesco accounts for one in five pounds spent on the British high street and is widely recognized as a global pioneer in designing and operating a customer loyalty programme – the Tesco Clubcard. In running this programme Tesco knows more about the shopping habits of an individual customer than that individual customer can generally hope to know about herself. I have even heard an urban myth that Tesco can determine the likelihood of a woman being pregnant based on subtle changes to her purchasing behaviour before she perhaps suspects it herself. To be clear, I have no evidence that this is anything more than a myth, and retail analytics specialists tend to laugh off the idea when I put it to them, but I include it here because it's both entertaining and thought provoking.

So the default I presented above, where the data and information I create directly or indirectly through my use of products and services is private and mine, is not actually the default today. And I attribute this simply to the fact that the capability to collect large datasets from individuals' use of products and services has crept up on society, and a pervasive attitude towards this gentle evolution to date is summed up by the quote 'what's the harm?' I consider such a relaxed response to be complacent in the extreme. It is complacent of the consumer and citizen, and it is complacent and possibly arrogant of organizations. Let me be absolutely clear: such a gentle evolution is over. We have started an unprecedented explosion in the ways we can digitize everything we do, record every move we make, and if it is left unchecked that's exactly what will happen. It's exactly what *is* happening.

By now, many readers will have seen online display ads for items previously viewed on an unrelated website. One day I'm browsing information about a new digital camera, and the next day there it is, the exact make and model advertised to me as if by magic. Except that it's not magic, and many recipients of this targeted advertising do not feel that tingle of excitement from having witnessed a magic trick, but the tingle of concern that they've been watched. Unannounced.

The massive consumer outrage expressed in 2008 over secret trials BT plc conducted in 2007 of just such behavioural targeting technology from a company called Phorm is now considered legendary in the UK. Similar alarm is being expressed about services from a company called RapLeaf as I write. So how might we reconcile lending our voice to the uproar over BT's shenanigans before then popping to the supermarket with our Clubcard in hand?

I think this indicates that some implicit understanding is at work for customers participating in loyalty programmes. In other words, they haven't read the 'small print' but they have twigged that the data is being stored and used by the retailer, whereas no such implicit understanding was formed between BT and its customers. There was no equivalent piece of plastic being read at the point of sale. BT's customers were ignorant of what was going on and the resultant consumer backlash was vicious.

Do you want to invite such a response from your stakeholders? This is a core question for influence professionals. Let's first take a more detailed look at what we're talking about, and then take an example of the kind of technologies and capabilities that influence professionals must consider.

Digital detritus

Each and every one of us is going to be kicking off more data describing our use of digital products and services; what some refer to as our digital exhaust or digital footprint, which I prefer to call digital detritus. We referred to it earlier in the influence traceability quadrants in Table 5.3.

Detritus is a biological word for discarded organic matter, such as leaf litter for example, which is then decomposed by microorganisms and re-appropriated by animal and plant life. It is then interestingly analogous to our regard for, and treatment of, this data we're all shedding and the natural hunger to collect and digest it.

We collect the click path of visitors' interactions with our website today, but we can't yet access the data describing their use of physical products – but this is changing, as we've seen with the Internet of Things.

We can invite customers to share their location data with us via their mobile phones, but we can't yet help them to review their driving style or use of public transport. This is also changing. Electronic payment services such as London's Oyster Card allow the transport authorities to review customer journeys in the particulate or aggregate, therefore this data is available to share if and when demanded, and Fiat's Ecodrive facility already enables the drivers of some of its cars to collect driving information on a USB stick for subsequent sharing with Fiat and mutual analysis.

We can encourage the consumer to reap the anticipated advantages of greener products and services, but we can't identify the actual advantage they achieve and reflect it back at them. Until, of course, they have smart meters and a home appliance network, for example.

We can market a food product's expected role in a balanced diet, but not the specific role it plays in a particular household's diet. Until all food products entering a household can be logged easily, perhaps courtesy of RFID, or until customers are given joint access to, and possibly joint ownership of, loyalty programme data.

Browser history

Your browser history is the log that lists every webpage you visit. It's this list that enables modern browsers to suggest auto-completions for URLs as you enter them in the address bar. It's this list you might visit when you're trying to find that something or other you stumbled across the other day. It's this list that allows your browser to try to render unvisited links one way (underlined blue by default), and previously visited links another way (underlined purple by default), even though individual webpages and associated styling information may actually override these defaults.

Who owns your browser history?

As far as I'm concerned, my browser history is mine. My wife's browser history is hers. Your browser history is yours.

So here's a question you may or may not have ever asked yourself, depending on the focus of your job: Has your browser history been 'sniffed' at any time? Well you wouldn't know, I'm afraid.

It's been known for nearly a decade that the feature of a browser that conveniently tries to show visited and unvisited links differently (courtesy of your browser history) leaves that history open to being 'sniffed'. Specifically, if I want to know if you've visited a specific webpage before visiting my website, all I have to do is include a link to that webpage on my webpage and, with a little bit of code, I can get my webpage to tell me what colour your browser is trying to use to display the URL. Purple? Yes: then you've been there.

What's more, I can make sure you don't even see that I'm trying to display this link, or hundreds of others. In simple terms, a webpage layout is a grid with references setting how far from the left and how far down from the top something appears. If I set the horizontal position of the links to something like minus 999, it is effectively 'displayed' to the left of your visible screen, i.e. invisible to you.

Let's try it now. We can see it in a way that is plain and clear. Visit the over-exaggeratedly named www.whattheInternetknowsaboutyou.com and it will check to see which of some 5,000 popular websites your browser betrays you as having visited.[123] (I'm happy to point you to this harmless website as its *raison d'être* is simply to educate you about this matter.)

So, you're in marketing and PR and you want to close the loop. You want to determine whether all those places on the Web where you've managed to get exposure for your brand (paid and unpaid) actually drive people to look at your website. You want to see which of your competitors' websites a visitor to your website has looked at previously. You want to check if visitors to your website hang out at certain websites. Basically, you want to trace influence.

Of course, if they landed on your website because they'd clicked links to one of your webpages at these places, then your Web analytics will log the referring webpages accordingly. But what if the visitor left a few days between going to these places, and therefore potentially seeing or reading stuff about you, and deciding to pop over to your website today?

Well, first up, congratulations on having the ambition to close the loop, to trace influence, but is this the way to do it? Is this ethical? After all, you're sniffing behind your visitors' backs, which actually isn't all that pleasant a metaphor.

Browser history sniffing is included here as just one example of the armoury of technologies available to marketers today. If this intrigued you, you'll find the blog post *The Data Bubble* by Doc Searls, July 2010, fascinating.[124] We met Doc in this book's Introduction as the co-author of the *Cluetrain Manifesto* and we'll meet him again later in this chapter when we refer to vendor relationship management. His post was inspired by a series in the *Wall Street Journal* chillingly titled *What They Know*.[125]

A question of policy

The browser history example prompts questions on three levels. On the lowest level: does your organization have a policy towards the use of browser sniffing? At a higher level: does your organization have a policy that defines explicitly your approach to all such data-harvesting possibilities? And at the highest level: does your organization have a privacy and data ownership policy, and if so is it suitable for the whole topic of tracing influence and the related technologies, present and future?

From my experience, if your organization has yet to think this through, let alone crystallize and communicate it in its policy, then you are in the clear majority. And where privacy policies do exist, most do not cover the ramifications of the kind of capabilities we're debating here.

A question of leadership

If there's one word that sums up our journey in the last 10 years, it's *authenticity*. As David Meerman Scott writes in *The New Rules of Marketing and PR*: 'People want authenticity, not spin.' James Gilmore and Joseph Pine, the authors of *Authenticity: What Consumers Really Want*[126] put it simply: '. . . consumers crave what's authentic . . . the more contrived the world seems, the more we all demand what's real.'

And interpreting the *Oxford English Dictionary*, authenticity refers to having the quality of an emotionally appropriate, significant, purposive, and responsible mode of human life.

Here, then, is an idea. If you want to know where people have been before they got to you, and you want to close the loop, and inform your marketing research and trace influence, why not just ask them nicely? You could even offer something useful to them in return. Why not say something like:

> Hi, thanks for dropping by. Ask any company and they'll say you dropping by is important to them, but we feel more strongly about it. We really want to understand what makes you tick so that we can do better at developing our products and services, and so that we can improve our ability to listen and understand your needs and answer any questions you might have.
>
> Knowing if you've been to a few dozen specific websites before coming here today would help us a lot, but if you don't want to, that's no problem at all. If you do, we'll be able to share with you how your potential trips to these websites compare to others who've shared this information with us, and perhaps there's a great site or two in there you've yet to discover!

> Just click here and we'll check your browser history now (or click here to find out how this is done, which websites we're interested in, and how our privacy policy guides our use of this capability).

Here's another scenario. Imagine that you're a mobile telephone network operator. Right now, you own the data describing the customer's use of your network. What competitive advantage might be had by reversing that situation, by transferring ownership to the customer – on the condition of service of course that you can have access to their data in order to determine billing and associated aspects of your service provision? And what if you gave the customer the tools to learn about her data, to download it and share it with whomever she wished. What might she learn about herself and her family? How might this data be mashed up? How much easier would it be to source the perfect tariff for the next year given the opportunity to share last year's data? If you think that sounds bad for business you're effectively saying that opacity is good. History has shown that walled gardens and other protective practices eventually crumble in competitive telephony markets.

What would this facility say about your respect for your customer? What does it communicate about the authenticity of your organization? What positive influence might this stance have on your stakeholders to the advantageous pursuit of your organizational objectives? Of course, this considerable reputational fillip is accrued most to the first mover; the others are then just catching up in the eyes of the consumer.

The BT and Phorm example – plus the Facebook privacy backlashes of 2009 and 2010 – are sufficient evidence to me that no one can rely upon implicit acceptance. Things are changing too fast for that these days.

A potential privacy framework for the influence professional

Alan Westin's definition of privacy from 1967 has stood the tests of time as far as I'm concerned. He defines *privacy* as the ability to determine for ourselves when, how, and to what extent information about us is communicated to others.[127]

I presented a potential privacy framework at Internetome: the Internet of Things Conference, London 2010. It's a framework for influence professionals and their product development and delivery colleagues that puts the customer/citizen in charge as much as the laws of the land permit.

A similar framework may well be possible that pivots around co-ownership for example, i.e. data ownership by both the customer/citizen and the organization in question, but I'll postpone that because (a) I'd first like to understand readers' response to this framework, and (b) I have no legal training, and co-ownership becomes a little trickier to articulate. But perhaps most importantly, I believe that a future where so much data is collected about me and owned by others is nothing short of dystopian. And, at the risk of repeating myself, linearly extrapolating from today to tomorrow falls so far short of the reality we're considering here that it's not only useless but entirely misleading. This is much more than just a really big Clubcard. This involves every single thing you interact with logging some data about that interaction, and all the emergent insight and implications that come out of this unprecedented mixing and analysis of detailed, real-time data. And this isn't futurology; it has already begun – so, no, I'm not being alarmist.

I've heard Google's present capabilities described as the first real-time continuous global census, but we'll laugh at the paucity of current capabilities in a few years' time – or mourn the days.

The primary motivation for a common framework is simply that the consumer/citizen is going to be faced with such choices many times and for very many products and services, so a uniformity in the way the choices are presented benefits both sides of the transaction in terms of efficiency of communication and managed expectations. The product or service provider can simply reference its legal compliance with such a framework by use of the associated trademark and presentation of the familiar options. The product or service provider may choose not to make all the options available, of course, or price them differently, or provide different benefits at each level. Such things just become another aspect to consider in the prospective customer's purchase decisions.

The framework consists of four levels of data treatment in which the normal data protection laws of the land apply. In layman's terms these levels are:

1. *Delete* – delete at source without data collection where possible. If the data must be shared to enable service provision, I retain full ownership rights

and I want you to delete the data permanently at the soonest opportunity permissible under data retention laws

2. *Sustain* – I retain full ownership rights. Delete data as soon as possible while sustaining (i.e. without deleteriously affecting) product or service performance and in compliance with data retention laws

3. *Stats* – I retain full ownership rights. Delete data as soon as possible while sustaining (i.e. without deleteriously affecting) product or service performance and in compliance with data retention laws, maintaining only summary statistical records thereafter (e.g. average daily mileage travelled by car in August rather than the day-by-day mileage)

4. *Archive* – I retain full ownership rights. Keep the data in its most granular format for five years or that period required by data retention laws after which time I accept that you might delete the data on economic grounds on condition that summary statistic records are maintained.

From an information standpoint, information is quite clearly lost with the third option compared to the fourth, but this option enables customers / citizens to retain the flavour and practicability of their data without effectively leaving their DNA all over it, so to speak.

How might such an information loss be governed? Should a mobile operator, for example, store the time the customer spent on the phone in minutes per day, per week, or per month? Some statistical standards can be set and a simplified version might have the form shown in Table 8.1.

Table 8.1: Example statistical rules for information loss

Typical data points per annum	Aggregation period
<25	Year
25–100	Quarter
101–500	Month
501–2,000	Week
2,001–10,000	Day
10,000 +	Hour

So far the customer / citizen has had to make one choice, now there are two others to make:

- How might this data be shared with third parties?

There are three possible answers to this question: first – no sharing; second – anonymous sharing only, essential for example to contextual advertising or aggregate analysis; third – named sharing (i.e. not anonymous), relating again to third-party marketing potential.

And lastly:

- Does the customer have a streams bank with which she wants to store the data?

What's a streams bank? It's the moniker I've given the service with the primary purpose of collecting all your digital detritus, all your so-called life streams of data, in one place on your behalf and giving you the power to analyse and visualize it all (. . . and streams bank sounds much nicer than detritus bank).

A streams bank archives the minutiae of your life, if you so wish. The service may offer suggestions or advice in decision-making, and perhaps it may even be relied upon to make certain decisions for you autonomously.

A streams bank may be a paid for service, or it may offer you the service for free should you permit it to share the data, anonymously or named, or in the aggregate, with others for marketing and marketing research purposes. Come to think of it, in a free market with appropriate demand, it might end up paying you. The streams bank will enable its customers to debunk false claims made by marketers, and test adherence to service level agreements, and it will also likely be the broker of your attention should the so-called attention economy emerge in full.[128]

A streams bank may also perform an altruistic role by enabling, for example, analysis of the way we all live together in order to re-engineer aspects of society to have less impact on the environment, subject to each customer's opt-in.

Variations on this idea are under development around the world, many originating from, or inspired by, the vendor relationship management (VRM) project,[129] which is run by Doc Searls as a research and development project of the Berkman Center for Internet & Society at Harvard University. It explores how customers may be given the same capabilities in managing their relationships with vendors as vendors have for managing customers` relations (using customer relationship management, CRM, systems).

The VRM team refers to a personal data store. The Mine Project aims to help individuals to take charge of their own data, and arrange it and share it according to their needs, without involving a third party.[130] The Kantara Initiative describes its goal as "to identify and document the use cases and scenarios that illustrate the various subsets of individual-driven information sharing, the benefits therein, and specify the policy and technology enablers that should be put in place to enable this information to flow".[131]

What might a privacy framework look like? Figure 8.1 summarizes the one we've developed in this chapter so far. The framework consists of eight options, each of which may be banked: delete, sustain, stats-none, archive-none, stats-anon, archive-anon, stats-named, archive-named.

One can now envisage every single or group of products and services having a selector dial with eight positions, dictating how the customer wishes to treat the associated data. Of course, the dial won't be physical; it will be virtual instrumentation on the user interface to the product or service, and accessible from any authorized screen-based computing device. And yes, your toilet will have a user interface! Your electricity supply will have a user interface, as will your washing machine, bedside light, shoes, basketball hoop, dog, refuse and front door.

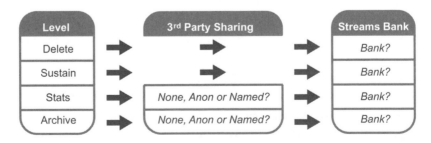

Figure 8.1: Potential privacy framework

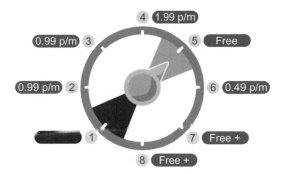

Figure 8.2: An example privacy dial

Figure 8.2 shows an example dial. This dial is for a service that needs access to historic data to function, so the first position isn't available – conveyed by having that position 'greyed out' – and summary information about the costs and benefits are listed next to each dial position.

Of course, those who decide to take up the services of a streams bank will need to tell the bank in a similar way how they would like it to treat the data. Should the bank adopt the policy you selected on the dial for the supplier of the product or service, or await your instructions on a case-by-case basis, or defer to an overarching policy that you've already defined with it?

Buyer marketing

We referenced the *Cluetrain Manifesto* from 1999 in the Introduction, positing that the Internet equilibrates the balance of power between the megacorp and the little consumer. The social Web has indeed facilitated the rebalancing of the respective share of voice during the first decade of the century by helping consumers to come together to exchange perspectives and experiences. The collective voice is heard.

Sometimes the collective voice is sufficiently loud and assertive that organizations have no choice but to improve their standards or change course but, with the exception of greater pricing transparency and price comparison capabilities, the direction of marketing and commerce remains unchanged.

The organization invests in helping you to understand why its products or service are worth buying (or point of view worth buying into) versus the competition, and the consumer navigates all the competing voices in making a purchase decision.

However, streams banks give rise to something I call buyer marketing, which is similar to what the VRM initiative refers to as a personal RFP[132] (request for proposal) and what Scott Adams, the creator of Dilbert, has recently labelled broadcast shopping.[133] This marks the point at which individuals can market their needs or desires, either directly or anonymously, via a streams bank or other broker, to organizations interested in meeting that need or desire.

Why the slightly different turns of phrase? Well, I'm happier that a buyer marketing his need leaves the speed or inevitability of a purchase a little more open ended, and the general public knows what both a 'buyer' and 'marketing' mean. RFP, on the other hand, is very much an industrial procurement acronym, possibly implying a predetermined course of action and timeline.

And 'broadcast' definitely doesn't sit well with my protocol-obsessed perspective. Buyer marketing is more multicast – a term describing the distribution of a message to a defined set of recipients as opposed to anyone and everyone who's listening. But I'm not that hung up on the terminology; it's the possibility and inevitability that matters.

While many of us have developed the remarkable ability to block the majority of adverts from our consciousness (what's the last banner ad you can recall?), the advent of buyer marketing will undoubtedly take this capability up a notch once each of us feels confident in our ability to pull customized 'tenders' to us on demand for anything and everything we can imagine.

Lastly, you might be interested to know that while the idea of buyer marketing reverses the normal marketing mechanism, one thing does not necessarily get flipped – identity. With an intermediary such as a streams bank working on her behalf, the prospect can elect to remain completely anonymous to you. If your product or service doesn't naturally need the customer to declare her identity, you might consider it your job as a marketer (influencer) to persuade her to part with this information through the provision of some great post-sales benefits, for example, so that you can hope to build a lifelong relationship.

Knowing what it all means

You may have come across the DIKW hierarchy. It goes by various names, including the knowledge hierarchy and wisdom hierarchy. The Wikipedia page on the topic makes for interesting reading, but for now suffice it to say it goes something like this:

- *Data* – discrete, objective facts, signals or symbols devoid of context and interpretation and therefore of no meaning or value.
- *Information* – the result of structuring or organizing data in such a way as to give it meaning and relevance for a specific purpose or in a specific context.
- *Knowledge* – the result of structuring or organizing information in such a way that it helps to form a framework for the incorporation of further information and aids the evaluation of the world, accruing experience, expertise and know-how.
- *Wisdom* – my favourite definition of wisdom is the ability to make information super-useful. Often, wisdom is described as an amalgam of knowledge and judgement, resulting in 'know-why' in the form of 'why do' (rather than in the form of 'why is', which is information).

The journalist and broadcaster Miles Kington is attributed with the saying: 'Knowledge is knowing that a tomato is a fruit. Wisdom is knowing that a tomato doesn't belong in a fruit salad.' I'm not so sure. To me the first is information, the latter is knowledge, but this just exemplifies that the hierarchy is a bit blurry sometimes.

Nevertheless I raise DIKW because it is so much a part of the daily trials and tribulations of the influence professional. Data is abundant today, and we've already seen what's just around the corner; a prospect Bret Swanson of the Discovery Institute calls the exaflood, a neologism referencing the exabyte (a million terabytes, or a billion gigabytes), which is quite a lot of data indeed.

During our review of semantic Web analysis we discussed the capabilities and limits of semantic analysis in automating the analysis of more brand references on the social Web than could ever be digested manually; a process of transforming data into information into knowledge. The influence professional must keep a beady eye on how well her organization is gathering data in each of the influence flows and transforming it accordingly, being sure to upgrade the capabilities as and when needed and feasible, and attributing appropriate caution to the application of knowledge that might have been consolidated from incomplete data or with a less than perfect process.

In the Introduction I gave a brief definition of Web 3.0, which I'll expand on now.

If Web 2.0 is all about (user-generated) content and community participation, Web 3.0 is about the Web itself understanding the meaning of all the content and participation. Indeed, the Web becomes a universal medium for the exchange of data, information and knowledge.

Web 3.0 is more accurately called the semantic Web, although the phrase Web of Data is increasingly popular. To clarify the terms here, semantic Web analysis is a term encompassing techniques to infer meaning in (including the sentiment of) contributions made to the social Web (Web 2.0). The semantic Web (Web 3.0) allows for that meaning to be built in to all published data including, potentially, those contributions.

The semantic Web includes a vision known as Linked Data, which in simple terms allows data to be described with reference to universally available common vocabularies, and considerable work is going on around the world on defining these vocabularies and linking datasets accordingly. Figure 8.3 diagrammatically represents a snapshot of this interlinking as of September 2010.[134]

Do you recall some of those oft-repeated diagrams in Web 2.0 books and training? Well expect to see this one, and possibly updates to it if they continue to fit on one page, many times in the coming years. It's probably too detailed to be legible in print here (you can follow the link in the endnotes) but the message it conveys isn't contained in its text but in the number of data sources (circles) and the extent of the interlinking.

When the team at Wiley and I were discussing what should be included in this book there was some concern that reference to such technologies might be a case of me wearing my technology and engineering hat more than my marketing and PR hat. But in the end the conclusion was resolute: Web 3.0 had to make the final edit because it is happening *now* at the BBC, Wikipedia, Google and within the UK and US governments, to name just a

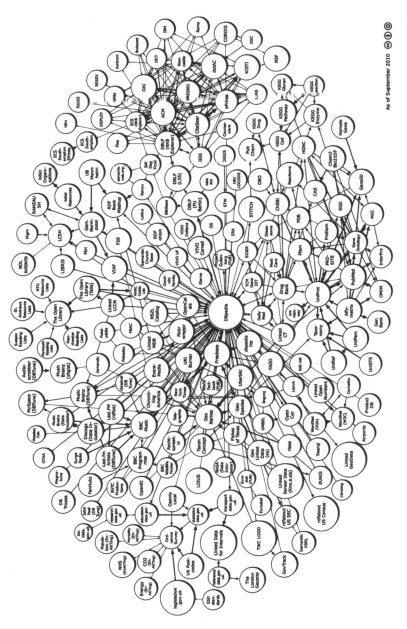

Figure 8.3: The LinkedOpenData Project interlinked datasets, September 2010

few of the hundreds of organizations, and moreover I hope I can convey what it means without resort to technical jargon or acronyms.

It is significant that The International Press Telecommunications Council is also using Web 3.0. The Council announced in April 2010 the official launch and widespread adoption of its G2 family of news exchange standards supported by Agence France-Presse, Associated Press, dpa, The Press Association, and Thomson Reuters. G2 contains some Web 3.0 components.

For those readers who'd like to delve a little more deeply, I can point you to the presentation I delivered at the CIPR, August 2010, *Intro to Web 3.0 and the Internet of Things.*[135]

Google loves the semantic Web

GoodRelations is the name of one of those universal vocabularies, specifically formed to describe aspects of ecommerce (despite sounding like a great name for a PR vocabulary). During the Search Engine Strategies 2009 conference in Chicago, Jay Myers, Lead Web Development Engineer for Best Buy, reported that applying GoodRelations improved the rank of the respective pages in Google tremendously, and increased traffic to Best Buy store webpages by 30%.[136]

One might interpret this boost to Best Buy's PageRank as Google's way of saying: 'Hey, this semantic Web thing, specifically this Linked Data initiative, is incredibly useful, so here's our way of showing our appreciation for your early adoption Best Buy. Any more for any more?' Google now provides information on how to publish content semantically in its Webmaster Central forum in the *Creating Google-Friendly Sites* section.

As of May 2009 Google uses semantically marked up content to create what it calls 'rich snippets' in its search results.[137] You'll probably have seen them if Google is your search engine of choice. An example is shown in Figure 8.4.

HTC Desire mobile phone review - Pocket-lint ☆
★★★★★ Review by Chris Hall - 29 Mar 2010
29 Mar 2010 ... HTC Desire mobile phone - The ace in HTC's Android pack? full review.
www.pocket-lint.com/review/4694/htc-desire-mobile-phone-review - Cached

Figure 8.4: Example of a Google rich snippet

In this example, the rich snippet is possible only because the data source, Pocket-lint, marks its content up semantically and to a standard recognized by Google, lending the star rating meaning that Google can understand and use.

There's no influence without meaning

That's enough on the semantic Web for now. I've tried to think of a catchy way to conclude this section to live up to the incredibly high standard I set with 'there's money in them thar flows'. How about: 'There's no influence without meaning'?

Actually, before we conclude this introduction to Web 3.0, I'll leave you with some homework if I may to put this whole section into context. It shows you how, by embedding meaning into datasets, we can follow these links and join the dots and explore the world in unprecedented ways. Movie databases are one of the first data sources to get the Linked Data treatment, so let's employ a semantic Web browser to explore the connections and relationships between two different movies. Here's the step-by-step guide:

1. Visit http://relfinder.dbpedia.org/relfinder.html
2. Type 'Million Dollar Baby' in the first box – selecting the first result the engine finds
3. Type 'Letters from Iwo Jima' in the second box – again selecting the first result the engine finds
4. Now click 'Find Relations'.

. . . and sit back and feel the power of the semantic Web. Click the boxes with rounded corners to explore specific relationships. And of course, browse the connections between other films, or actors. And imagine the (influence) possibilities if all your data and the data of others was as easy to link and traverse.

Summary

- Smartphones are the most personal of all digital devices – critical 'influence devices'

- Smartphones appear to be the domain in which permission marketing is most critical
- The Internet of Things exists already, and is about to become an incredible force for influence professionals to reckon with
- The Internet of Things opens up new product and service development and marketing opportunities
- Who owns the data? We are considering a dystopian scenario
- Is there a leadership opportunity to demonstrate authenticity?
- Is the new privacy framework workable in your organization?
- Are your products and services suitable for application of a privacy dial?
- Buyer marketing describes individuals marketing their needs or desires, either directly or anonymously via a streams bank or other broker, to organizations interested in meeting that need or desire
- The semantic Web (also known as Web 3.0) is about the Web itself understanding the meaning of content and social participation – the Web becomes a universal medium for data, information and knowledge exchange
- There's no influence without meaning.

Our next chapter is short but important, aiming simply to reframe marketing and PR in the light of the Influence Scorecard. We won't summarize the next chapter therefore, but rather proceed straight on to defining the role of Chief Influence Officer and the influence professional.

9

For convenience I'll repeat here one of the definitions of marketing and one of public relations we met earlier.

- *Marketing is the process by which companies create value for customers and build strong customer relationships in order to capture value from customers in return.*
- *Public relations is the focus on two-way communication and fostering of mutually beneficial relationships between an organization and its publics.*

In my words, marketing describes the process of making and growing a profitable market, in partnership with public relations' mutual alignment of the organization with its stakeholders. (Substitute the phrase 'profitable market' when your organization has a different primary motivation.)

Influence performance management

In our framework, I posit that marketing and public relations describe approaches to particular aspects and subsets of the Six Influence Flows and the Influence Scorecard, and have been defined in the context of 20th-century technology, 20th-century media, and 20th-century articulation of and appreciation for business strategy.

We must now consider (in the order we've covered them here) the ramifications of the social Web, social Web analytics, complexity, modern strategy methodologies and business performance management, mobile and the

Internet of Things, privacy, streams banks, buyer marketing, and the semantic Web. We must consider that there is influence in everything an organization does, and increasingly in everything consumers and citizens do and every 'thing' they interact with.

Media has most definitely evolved, as have the ways in which we contemplate, design, communicate and execute strategy. And rather than technological evolution, we're plainly in the midst of a technological revolution.

We have no choice, then, but to reframe marketing and PR in the bigger picture of the Influence Scorecard, a reframing in the context of 21st-century technology, 21st-century media and disintermediation, and 21st-century articulation of and appreciation for business strategy. Below is how I present it.

The ease and effectiveness with which we can manage and learn from influence flows is integral to the process by which customers, citizens and all stakeholders interact with organizations and governments to broker mutually valuable, beneficial relationships.

10

Let me generalize. Marketing is too hit and miss. Advertising is in spasm. Public relations is polarized, with a minority that 'get it' and a majority that don't know they don't. Customer service is drowning. The 'digital' slash 'social' set are trying hard to live up to the false promise they promised. The Chief Exec is frustrated that things just aren't gelling. And almost everyone is inwardly focused on the current recessionary (or at least 'non-boom') climate, this month's costs and cash flows.

Is this fair? No, I said I was generalizing. But I have spoken with quite a few board directors from different disciplinary backgrounds over the last few years who hold at least one of these views about the other disciplines, and not too rarely about their own.

Confusion reigns. We have SEO shops issuing press releases (and running reputational risks[138]), advertising firms recruiting PR consultants,[139] PR firms brushing up their SEO,[140] and a 'media buying shop' being awarded a major digital PR contract.[141] Many organizations, not just end-users, appear to be suffering so-called social network fatigue.

Some baggage handlers break a guitar and some customer service staff claim ignorance, and then it's all hands fighting the fire.[142] Nokia's failure to understand changes in its market are partially attributed by *Bloomberg BusinessWeek* to it being in Finland, "that meant it wasn't in the mix of innovative ideas, which would have forced it to question its assumptions – and watch its back – every day".[143] Separately, a *Harvard Business Review* article[144] acclaims Nokia for its success in Asia in bringing the customer into the product design process.

As I concluded in the previous chapter, we need to reframe things in the context of 21st-century technology, 21st-century media and disintermediation, and 21st-century articulation of, and appreciation for, business strategy.

It's time for the Chief Influence Officer to enter the frame, ably assisted by a crack team of influence professionals putting the Influence Scorecard to work. It's time to make the art and science of influencing and being influenced a core organizational discipline. It's time to get your organization a consistent, cohesive, coherent and measurable influence strategy.

The Chief Influence Officer

Unsurprisingly, perhaps, the Chief Influence Officer's role consists partly of an amalgam of current role descriptions, and therefore of various person specifications / traits, and partly distinct characteristics demanded of the distinctive new role. Before defining the role, the skills and person specification, let's take a quick look at how some existing titles are said to be evolving, and a look at two relatively new C-suite titles.

Chief Communications Officer

It's only the most proven and persistent Heads of Communications that get the C-title, and only then in organizations with boards that pay a little more attention to good governance and have a better understanding of the wider and deeper strategic role the CCO plays. Reassuming my mode of generalizing: all other organizations are populated by CxOs who consider the Head of Comms to be the 'head of press releases, other media relations and urgent responses', or perhaps actually have a comms head that pigeonholes himself and his team as such.

While definitions of public relations vary, as we took time to review towards the beginning of the book, too few practitioners get the opportunity to deliver the benefits of the full gamut of the public relations role definition in my experience, or are under-qualified to do so from a lack of continuous professional development. I've claimed that PR professionals today do not generally attain an appropriate balance of 1st and 3rd flows, with the organization's influence over its stakeholders given considerably more time and effort than the reciprocal.

How might the role be evolving?

In an interview I recorded with the prominent PR thought leader and author Brian Solis,[145] our conversation turned to the new PR practitioner Brian emphasized the left-brained aspects demanded of today's practitioner – the data and research skills – and the key role the practitioner must play in 'the socialization of business'. I asked Brian how he thought PR directors with 20+ years' experience in traditional media could best transform their skill set to the digital age:

> I'm not sure every PR practitioner is going to make the transition to social and that's not necessarily a bad thing either. . . . We do need a hybrid of professional who can come in and lead at the top-level [to establish] structure and process and governance.

Perhaps Brian's hybrid isn't too distant a cousin to our influence professional?

And earlier I quoted a similar interview with Katie Delahaye Paine of KD Paine & Partners during which she also declared that the new PR professional must graduate with a solid foundation in statistics.[146]

Jay O'Connor, CIPR President 2010, emphasizes the need for CCOs / Directors of Public Relations or Corporate Communications to acquit themselves in the wider context of organizational leadership. She is a Chartered PR Practitioner and a Chartered Director of the UK's Institute of Directors – so she practises what she preaches. Jay believes that more senior PR professionals must prepare themselves

> to talk the language of the board, with a particular emphasis on strategy formulation, organizational structure, planning, measurement and organizational learning – in short, to play a full rather than simply functional role in the boardroom.

The 2007 report from the Arthur W. Page Society, *The Authentic Enterprise*,[147] identifies four new leadership priorities and skills demanded of the Chief Communications Officer:

- Leadership in defining and instilling company values
- Leadership in building and managing multi-stakeholder relationships
- Leadership in enabling the enterprise with 'new media' skills and tools and
- Leadership in building and managing trust, in all its dimensions.

To repeat a previous conclusion: 'our behaviours, manifest in influencing and being influenced through products and services and customer relations and communications and interactions of all kinds, accumulate to form a reputation and a degree of trustworthiness in people's minds, and to establish a level of significance in people's lives.' So it seems that the 2nd and 4th new leadership priorities listed here play well into the Influence Scorecard, and it will be the uncommon influence strategy that doesn't require emphasis on communicating values and employing new media.

Can the Head of Communications morph into the role of Chief Influence Officer? The best can, if they're suitably left-brain capable and willing and able to run headlong into a completely new scope replete with new learning curves and organizational resistance.

Chief Marketing Officer

What might we learn from some recent commentary about the new demands of CMOs?

In the foreword to the 2010 *Marketing Metrics: The Definitive Guide to Measuring Marketing Performance*,[148] John A. Quelch, Lincoln Filene Professor of Business Administration and Senior Associate Dean for International Development, Harvard Business School, writes:

> . . . many corporate boards lack the understanding to evaluate marketing strategies and expenditures. Most directors – and a rising percentage of Fortune 500 CEOs – lack deep experience in this field.
>
> Marketing executives, for their part, often fail to develop the quantitative, analytical skills needed to manage productivity. Right-brain

thinkers may devise creative campaigns to drive sales but show little interest in the wider financial impact of their work. Frequently, they resist being held accountable even for top-line performance, asserting that factors beyond their control – including competition – make it difficult to monitor the results of their programs.

... As I concluded in [a recent article in the *Wall Street*] *Journal*:

'Today's boards want chief marketing officers who can speak the language of productivity and return on investment and are willing to be held accountable. In recent years, manufacturing, procurement and logistics have all tightened their belts in the cause of improved productivity. As a result, marketing expenditures account for a larger percentage of many corporate cost structures than ever before. Today's boards don't need chief marketing officers who have creative flair but not financial discipline. They need ambidextrous marketers who offer both.'

This ambidexterity that Quelch calls for really makes sense to me. He is saying that the modern CMO must at once have empathy with the art and emotion of communication, married with the rigour of scientific management.

An assertion is made in the 2007 paper from the Chartered Institute of Marketing, *Tomorrow's World: Re-evaluating the Role of Marketing*,[149] that it is only natural for specialism to occur as a discipline becomes more sophisticated and knowledge accrues. Indeed, the paper refers briefly to the Renaissance and how it was considered normal for one individual to be engrossed in chemistry, biology and physics; drawing, painting and dissecting – a breadth that would be impossible today of course.

Increasingly, it's difficult for a marketer to attempt to be expert in all the areas we currently define as 'marketing'. One of the problems with the status of marketing is that a creative marketer is criticized for not being sufficiently metrics-oriented; whereas a good number cruncher is also expected to be a disruptive thinker.

The paper takes a stab at dividing the marketing domain into three broad paths:

- *Science* – R&D, segmentation, research, analysis, statistics, web strategy, metrics, technology, data and information
- *Arts* – Branding, advertising, communications. By making this area discrete, we replace the disadvantage of this area being perceived as the whole of marketing, with the advantage of it being regarded as a specialism
- *Humanities* – Social, ethical, cause-related, not-for-profit, triple bottom line [people, planet, profit]. Includes business sustainability, public sector and social marketing.

Like the Chief Communications Officer, the best, left-brain biased CMOs will be primary candidates for CInflO.

Chief Information Officer

Who would have thought that I would turn to the Chief Information Office next? Well, for a start, the CMO Council, Business Performance Innovation Network, and Accenture Interactive. The introduction to their fascinating collaborative October 2010 report, *The CMO-CIO Alignment Imperative: Driving Revenue through Customer relevance*,[150] entailing interviews with more than 330 global marketing executives and 313 global IT and information systems executives, declares:

> Marketers must seize the opportunity to more effectively engage with customers across a growing multiplicity of touch-points and channels, to more finely tune, target and personalize communications, to more deeply embed data-driven insight into every interaction and process, and to increase the productivity, ROI and measurability of marketing. But, to truly be successful, marketers can't do it alone. Enter the imperative for alignment, collaboration and integration with the CMO's greatest ally: the CIO.

The research found that two-thirds of CIOs and half of CMOs consider the entire customer experience to be underpinned and shaped by technology. And just over half of both groups believe that access to customer intelligence is critical to competitive advantage. The most demanded technologies relate to day-to-day marketing operations and CRM, and the idea that all that the CMO and CIO have to talk about are websites and email is resigned to history. They must work together on everything from database marketing, customer loyalty strategy, real-time programme measurement and social Web analytics.

Sixty-nine per cent of CMO respondents believe they have primary responsibility over digital marketing strategy, with just 19% considering the CIO and team to be important in this regard. Compare this to the finding that the majority (58%) of IT execs believe they are the champions of digital marketing, although half also credit the CMO.

How about the potential for that 'Awesome Analytics Advantage' we discussed earlier? Well, it appears to be at an early stage. Only about 1 in 12 respondents claimed their company has integrated its online and offline analytic capabilities. More alarmingly, 86% of marketers and 90% of IT execs can't yet claim to have well-integrated online analytics.

The report makes three recommendations:

1. Collaborate to communicate – pivoting around a 'unified view of outcomes', 'a shared language of business, goals and success'.
2. Start at minute one, not mission critical stages – 'create a roadmap . . . drawing from the strengths and intelligence of both marketing and IT'.
3. Don't test so long that you fail to invest – 'you must define where and how technology impacts the business and the customer engagement'.

And in the report's conclusion:

> The merged goals of both IT and marketing must rely on a unifying rallying cry around relevance. . . . There are riches to be won through this partnership. The challenge will be developing the skills, conversations, strategies and willingness to achieve true alignment and partnership.

We've already discussed this word 'relevance' of course (in the chapter on 'Influence') and we concluded that the better we are at influencing and being influenced, the more will our stakeholders perceive us to be relevant, resonant and accessible. Therefore, if you don't mind me swapping 'relevance' for 'influence' in the report's conclusion, it seems that the report's strong support for a more synchronized and coherent collaboration between the CMO and CIO might be interpreted to mean that the authors of the report would endorse at least a significant fraction of the Chief Influence Officer's remit. I can also only interpret the report's references to outcomes, goals, roadmap, alignment and riches to be as close to a ringing endorsement of the Influence Scorecard as one might find ahead of publishing this book.

Chief Operations Officer

I consider that the COO is the title here with the biggest gap between the incumbent's facility to influence and be influenced, and most incumbents' active recognition of that fact. Quality, efficiency, costs, resourcing, scheduling, alignment and skilling are all words that a COO would utter unprompted in describing the role to the uninitiated – but rarely *influence*.

By definition, the majority of a typical organization's staff comes under the COO's charge, a critical stakeholder group of itself, and a group most likely – purely by dint of numbers – to interact most with customers, suppliers, partners and the wider community. The staff's interpersonal communication skills and the processes they design and execute hour-by-hour can delight or frustrate the staff itself and all those other stakeholder groups.

It's noteworthy that it's simply misguided to believe that if the operations strategy is executed to plan, the influence aspects of operations will look after themselves. Without the cascade of an influence strategy into the operations strategy, and without the alignment of strategy mapping and scorecard construction, excelling at influence remains as likely to happen by itself as total quality management or just-in-time deliveries. That is, no chance.

The COO and CInflO must be close allies.

Chief Customer Officer

An article in January 2010's *Harvard Business Review*, Rethinking Marketing,[151] gets straight to the crux of the matter as far as its authors' vision for the Chief Customer Officer role is concerned:

> To be sure, most companies use customer relationship management and other technologies to get a handle on customers, but no amount of technology can really improve the situation as long as companies are set up to market products rather than cultivate customers. To compete in this aggressively interactive environment, companies must shift their focus from driving transactions to maximizing customer lifetime value. That means making products and brands subservient to long-term customer relationships. And that means changing strategy and structure across the organization – and reinventing the marketing department altogether.

The authors believe that the majority of C-suites just pay lip service to customer relationships while continuing to prioritize sales, yet leadership is required of the C-suite to shift the focus of strategy, culture, structure and incentives from transactions to relationships.

The authors point out that Chrysler, Hershey's, Oracle, Samsung, Sears, United Airlines, Sun Microsystems, and Wachovia all have Chief Customer Officers, and the title has grown 10-fold to 300 incumbents in the last seven years. However, they also point out that the role is too frequently ill-defined and currently has the shortest tenure in the C-suite. There appears, then, to be a substantial gulf between reality and the role the authors conceive: "a powerful operational position, reporting to the CEO. This executive is responsible for designing and executing the firm's customer relationship strategy and overseeing all customer-facing functions."

Why is there such a gulf?

I think the role struggles to justify itself in isolation from the rigour of the Influence Scorecard. The authors go so far as to identify potential KPIs, such as customer lifetime value (CLV) and 'customer equity', but any Chief Customer Officer plucking these KPIs from the ether – or, perhaps more kindly, with reference to what other Chief Customer Officers have adopted, without the studied cascade and organization-wide alignment we have here – will probably find any attempt to effect change futile. And such futility would explain the ephemerality of the role.

The Chief Customer Officer's role needs to be plugged into both the strategic lifeblood of the organization and the science of influence. If the role has neither, it may appear to other hardened C-titles to be no more than a fluffy and superfluous affirmation that the customer counts – which they'll avow to know already.

Chief Culture Officer

This CCO acronym is getting crowded – Communications, Customer and now Culture.

In *Chief Culture Officer: How to Create a Living, Breathing Corporation*,[152] anthropologist Grant McCracken urges boards to recognize the need for a "person who knows culture, both its fads and fashions, and its deep, enduring structures". You won't be surprised to hear that I concur with this point of view, and the book is a compelling read.

McCracken makes the case for corporations 'reading' the culture around them in the way that both Martha Stewart and Apple's Steve Jobs are renowned, for example. Interestingly, he believes that such skills can be nurtured, and are reproducible.

I'm less convinced of the likely success of Chief Culture Officers in representing their domain around the board table – a table at which the Chief Communications and Chief Marketing Officers still too frequently struggle to command respect, or at least acquit themselves measurably. I see such a role as critical but as a component of the Chief Influence Officer's team rather than a C-title in its own right. Please don't think this a case of C-suite Top Trumps™ however; it is not.

Other C-suite titles

Leaving aside the Chief Happiness Officer, Chief Ninja and other titles towards the wackier end of the spectrum, the Wikipedia entry for corporate titles[153] lists 50 at the time of writing. While I'll reassert that there's influence in everything, some titles that we have not already discussed but jump out most in our context are:

- Chief Brand Officer
- Chief Data Officer

- Chief Human Resources Officer
- Chief Knowledge Officer
- Chief Learning Officer
- Chief Networking Officer (as in human networking, not computing)
- Chief Privacy Officer
- Chief Procurement Officer
- Chief Sales Officer.

The Chief Influence Officer (CInflO)

Role

The role of Chief Influence Officer will be created in those organizations (or SBUs) with boards (or management teams) that recognize the potential for deriving competitive advantage in executing the Influence Scorecard, or who recognize the need to catch up with competing organizations that have already made the jump.

Early adopting organizations will be champions of the Balanced Scorecard or similar business performance management approach.

The incumbent is charged with making the art and science of influencing and being influenced a core organizational discipline – charged with executing the Influence Scorecard. They will be keen to network with peers in other organizations, to share best practice, to identify, refine and codify proven techniques, and to flag up unseen or unanticipated flaws in the processes described in this book – perhaps helping to document and discuss them on the accompanying website and in follow-up texts.

In my opinion, the role of Chief Influence Officer will be regarded as being on a par with the COO, as CEO-in-waiting.

Skills and person specification

Ideally, the Chief Influence Officer will have a varied background covering marketing, PR, customer service, HR, product development and operations – just the kind of trajectory frequently mapped out for 'future leader' types. They will probably have more experience in one or more of these over others of course, but will set out as a matter of urgency to orient themselves in the areas of the organization with which they have least experience, working hard to establish a thorough and lasting rapport with functional heads and all stakeholder groups. They will excel at interpersonal communication, inspire confidence and a can-do attitude, and know instinctively when to crack resistance one-on-one and when to draft in support from the CEO.

Given the not inconsiderable change management, collaboration and coordination challenges, boards will look in-house for candidates with extant strong organization-wide interpersonal relationships and a reputation for making change happen from both the hard and the soft side of things. Appropriate candidates will recognize that the task is not achievable alone, particularly without unanimous and unequivocal board support – which they will be intent on working hard to secure, if not already manifest by his or her appointment.

The candidates will be highly numerate, probably having taken a statistics or research methodologies component to their university degree.

They will be 'digitally native'. They will be curious and indefatigable by nature, and able to identify and exploit opportunities as rapidly as they identify and learn from failure.

They will be comfortable living simultaneously in both the extreme, unrelenting real-time, and the future two to four quarters hence.

They will have demonstrated a hunger for the C-suite or already be there, and will be intent on making the Chief Influence Officer title enduring. They will particularly relish the harsh, unflattering light thrown on previously opaque and unconnected aspects of the organization, and the boardroom accountability this allows them to enjoy and demands they live up to.

The Chief Influence Officer role requires ambidexterity.

On the left-brain side of things, the Chief Influence Officers get a distinct buzz from the numbers and the process of getting the numbers, and from learning from the numbers and putting that learning to productive use. They feel instant affinity with the thrust of this book: the recognition that things aren't working quite like they should right now; the imperative to integrate influence into business performance management; the opportunity to pare back the historic layers of structure, culture and processes, and build out anew; and to take command of the opportunities. They excel at both the analysis of complex situations and the synthesis of new processes.

On the right-brain side of things, they maintain a visceral sense of the human: for emotion expressed and contained; for the needs and desires of all stakeholder groups; for the creatively outstanding; and for the intangible interplay of brand values and associations. They have empathy for the organization as a living, breathing entity, in continual interaction and tension with its environs. They fully appreciate the change they are about to embark upon, how best to work with the CEO and other C-level colleagues, and how to communicate the transformation to their own team and wider organization and win their support. They will recognize why it's important to invest time ensuring that everyone appreciates their new or revised role and the refocused structure and influence culture around them.

While the requirement for deft change management skills is most obviously required of the first incumbents in order to make the transition to the Influence Scorecard, such skills remain key to subsequent incumbents, given their insight into the influence flows. There's less advantage in hyper-sensitizing the organization to its stakeholder relationships and the Six Influence Flows if the person at the centre of such operations cannot help to define the reflex – the responses the organization must explore, design and execute.

They will be skilled lateral thinkers, never afraid to ask 'stupid' questions.

As few candidates will bear such equilibrium of mind and capability, the majority of candidates will have a tendency towards the left-brain talents, selecting their team to counterbalance accordingly. I find it difficult to envisage the opposite working, especially if the bias away from left-brain talents is such that it impairs the incumbent's proficiency in systematically and scientifically transforming the organization's approach to influence. Perhaps a Chief Influence Officer with a right-brain tendency could be a suitable successor to the first left-brain tendency incumbent.

The influence professional

The influence professional works under the CInflO and, as you'd expect, doesn't quite have the breadth or depth of management or leadership qualities held by the CInflO. They may have jumped over to the influence discipline from marketing or PR or customer service, or perhaps they studied the Influence Scorecard at college should faculty thread it into syllabi in the years ahead.

An influence professional may be responsible for working with particular aspects of the business, such as operations or customer service or HR or analytics, ensuring strategic alignment, identifying and exploring opportunities for improvement, driving performance against the metrics, and helping the organization to transition its culture for influence success. As we discussed earlier, the team of influence professionals will attend to the roles mapped out for the Chief Customer Officer and the Chief Culture Officer.

The influence professional is an astute student of the big trends we covered earlier, and those of equivalent import in the unknown future, seeking to understand how they affect their organization's marketplace and how the organization might rise to the challenges and pursue the opportunities.

Organization structure – the office of influence performance management

I agree with the assertions of the CIM identified earlier in this chapter – that is, marketing requires greater specialization to maintain proficiency let alone to create competitive advantage; and the same applies to the influence processes. Actually, in my opinion, there are two extremes. Just as you may prioritize having the deepest domain expertise in government affairs or customer service, the Chief Influence Officer and team of influence professionals are expert in their generalist understanding of all the activities and parameters entailing influence flows. They are as comfortable discussing the latest thinking in resonance-based advertising on Twitter as they are reviewing the training and development programme for retail staff; as fluent in marketing research approaches as social Web analytics as corporate social responsibility as internal communications as contributing to the functional requirements definition of CRM and BI (business intelligence) systems.

On the face of it, the emergence of such 'expert generalists' accompanied by the deepening of specialist domain expertise leaves less room for those with mid-breadth and mid-depth outlook. It might well be that those who find themselves in such a position need to make a call as to whether to grow breadth or depth, but this will pivot on the degree to which an organization layers or rather delayers its structure.

As you'll recall, Kaplan and Norton have documented the formation of the office of strategy management, OSM – a consequence of a previously unmet requirement to assign ownership of responsibility for strategy. I consider this to be an interesting model for influence too as we must be looking here at some kind of matrix structure. For example, there will be operational activities over which the CInflO will want visibility and control because the activities play a vital role in the execution of the influence strategy. At the same time, there will be many other operational activities beyond the CInflO's concern. We cannot divorce these activities from each other, however, by assigning the first set to the CInflO and the latter to the COO as that would not only be artificial, it would be simply unworkable.

I believe we'll see the rise of something we might call the office of influence performance management (OIPM), run by the CInflO, taking responsibility for every aspect of the Six Influence Flows and the Influence Scorecard we've covered here, including:

- Defining the influence objectives
- Developing and articulating the influence strategy
- Mapping and communicating the influence strategy
- Representing influence within the OSM (with the CInflO taking the 'integrator' role)
- Constructing and maintaining the Influence Scorecard, including metric selection
- Facilitating the budget discussion, ensuring influence-related investment is apportioned in alignment with the influence strategy
- Reviewing structures and processes for fitness for purpose, defining the case for transformation as required to best pursue the influence strategy
- Reviewing external agency and partners for fitness for purpose, defining the case for review as required.

The OIPM will work hard to be seen to the rest of the organization as a productive partner. It will champion its role unceasingly but it will recognize that its role is best undertaken by working with, rather than against, other functional heads in trying to get the ever-challenging matrix of responsibilities working in the best interests of the organization. It will lean heavily on the objectivity of the Influence and Balanced Scorecards to guide behaviours transparently and apolitically.

Will marketing and PR continue to exist departmentally? Yes, for the time being. To demand that everything must change at once only invites failure and a volte-face to the comfort of traditional structure and process. Just as the operations team has domain over operations, and the HR team over human resources, marketing will continue to have domain over the product, price, place and promotion, in relation to the customer stakeholder, and PR over two-way communication and mutually beneficial relationships with all stakeholders. The OIPM will matrix into each one.

However, marketing, public relations and customer service will probably come directly under the domain of the CInflO in the longer term. Unlike other aspects of the business in which influence flows, these three areas pivot almost entirely around the flows of influence. We have reframed marketing and PR here in the context of the Influence Scorecard and 21st-century technology, media and disintermediation, and articulation of and appreciation for business strategy. Their ultimate absorption under the CInflO's domain is only logical, in my opinion. This may therefore entail the cessation of CMO and CCO roles, particularly if the CEO wishes to maintain a small C-suite.

We've seen the *Excellence* study's conclusion that excellent public relations does not come under the CMO in an integrated marketing communications environment or otherwise. I believe that our framework and the CInflO are just the unifying forces required to align and integrate marketing and public relations type activities once and for all. (Grunig *et al.* might still insist that the CInflO is a public relations expert, of course.)

External agency and partners

According to Steve Earl, Managing Director of Speed Communications (jointly with Stephen Waddington who we quoted earlier), the majority of organizations have no idea how to procure marketing and PR services, and I have to say he is not a lone voice in expressing such frustration. And I agreed with him again when he intimated that in-house marketing teams have hardly changed in three decades beyond recruiting some people with the word 'digital' in their job title. I feel his dissatisfaction that his team isn't always allowed to deliver the full benefits it could in every instance, in collaborating with the in-house team seamlessly. His sentiment to me in writing this book is simply: 'hope you've cracked it!'

One of the OIPM's responsibilities is to review existing agency and partners for their suitability in executing the influence strategy. The communication and training role of the OIPM extends beyond employees, and this is particularly pertinent during the early years when such discussion may be the first time an organization's partners encounter the Influence Scorecard. Of course, consultants are equally as likely to be the ones raising it with clients.

From an agency perspective, gone are the days when an ad agency can acceptably offer up one of their ad prescriptions, or a PR agency one of their standard media relations campaigns. Same old same old, in unaccountable isolation, at least in comparison to the Influence Scorecard.

So, in response to Steve's hopes for this framework, I believe that the organization operating the Influence Scorecard now knows precisely what it needs in measurable influence terms from agency, and beyond the norm, beyond marketing and beyond PR. This should therefore represent an exciting time for the agency and consultancy, offering fresh opportunities to design differentiation in a marketplace that has otherwise matured to almost bland saturation, and to do so accountably; to help to construct what might be referred to as an influence 'supply chain' as long as that term doesn't imply any asymmetry of influence flow.

My colleague Gabbi Cahane describes the new breed of agency:

> The 'agency of the future', engaged by the genuine influence profes-
> sional, will surely need to nurture not only the traditional creative
> and strategic skills expected as standard, but also the analytical,
> technological, entrepreneurial, financial, social, psychological, com-
> mercial, editorial, and experimental skills that drive organizations
> forward.

> The agency of the future will be a beautiful mutation continuously selecting the best DNA from the disciplines of influence – marketing and communications, operational and management consultancy, venture, investment, research, content creation, publishing, art and design – and constantly evolving to take advantage of their environment.

I also expect to see a new breed of consultancy coming to the fore with the specific purpose of facilitating clients' transition to the Influence Scorecard, and its successful continued operation. They'll be founded and staffed by people with appropriate backgrounds in marketing, public relations, customer service, operations, management consultancy and business performance management.

Summary

- We need to reframe things in the context of 21st-century technology, 21st-century media and disintermediation, and 21st-century articulation of and appreciation for business strategy
- Technology underpins this transformation and it has already been identified that the partnership between the CMO and Chief Information Officer must be nurtured
- The Chief Customer Officer and Chief Culture Officer roles have valid ambition but insufficient process to be viable – the roles will be covered by the CInflO's team
- The Chief Influence Officer (CInflO) is charged with making the art and science of influencing and being influenced a core organizational discipline; charged with executing the Influence Scorecard
- The COO and CInflO must be close allies, obviously
- Organizations already championing the Balanced Scorecard or similar business performance management approach will be the earliest to adopters of the Influence Scorecard
- The best, left-brain-oriented Chief Communications Officers and Chief Marketing Officers may be CInflO candidates

- The successful CInflO candidate has a varied background covering marketing, PR, customer service, HR, product development and operations – just the kind of trajectory frequently mapped out for 'future leader' types
- Candidates for the role will be in-house, with extant strong senior interpersonal relationships
- They will be highly numerate, digitally native, and ambidextrous thinkers – although probably left-brain biased
- The influence professional is an 'expert generalist' and an astute student of the big trends we've discussed here
- The CInflO heads up the Office of Influence Performance Management (OIPM)
- Marketing, PR and customer service will ultimately come under the CInflO's domain
- The transformation encompassed by the Influence Scorecard represents excellent opportunities for service differentiation by consultancies and agencies.

We've come to the end of the rethink described in this book's Introduction, and we have one last chapter on the next steps you might want to take now.

11

This chapter takes a quick look at the course of action an organization or SBU might take in considering and executing the Influence Scorecard. I'm assuming that one individual from that organization has just read this book, perhaps the CEO or CMO or CCO, and could now use a convenient checklist and action plan to kick things off.

We look at the prerequisites, the pre-board-approval actions, and the post-board-approval actions.

Prerequisites

To repeat an earlier statement, your organization will already champion the Balanced Scorecard or similar business performance management approach. While the Six Influence Flows stand alone to do with as you wish, to kick start your own rethink, the Influence Scorecard demands the same organizational discipline that was required to implement Kaplan and Norton's strategy maps and Balanced Scorecard in the first place, and demanded by its continued operation. If your organization doesn't employ the Balanced Scorecard but has similar processes, you will have to decide whether the degree of similarity and robustness is sufficient to warrant adapting the Influence Scorecard to meld appropriately. If your organization doesn't operate anything like the Balanced Scorecard, then it will need to explore this opportunity first.

Those organizations that are first to adopt the Influence Scorecard will typically emphasize a process strategy (seeking competitive advantage from operational excellence) and a customer-centricity (seeking competitive advantage from being better at placing the customer at the heart of the business). While the latter, seemingly, de-emphasizes the other stakeholder groups that are counter to our framework, I take it to be a good omen that the team running the organization in question gets this sort of thing.

Pre-board-approval actions

Being of critical strategic importance, the same degree of board and management team consensus and support is required here as for any major new strategic imperative. This book is, therefore, the best place to start – communicating the reasons for developing the new framework to your colleagues, and presenting the framework itself and the accompanying manifold implications. The accompanying website may also prove useful.

You may then wish to embark on a feasibility study, just as you would for any other initiative. The study will aim to:

- Document the current situation as pertaining to the consistency and coherence or otherwise with which your organization deals with the Six Influence Flows today.
- Describe the characteristics of the likely manifestation of the Influence Scorecard in your particular circumstances.
- Qualify and quantify the most significant benefits a transition to the Influence Scorecard should facilitate in your pursuit of your organization's vision.
- Qualify and quantify the most significant obstacles to making the transition successfully, including both hard and soft factors.
- Outline the project plan required to make the transition, identifying the resources required, the dependencies and the timeline.

Post-board-approval actions

Extant texts and case studies for the transition to the Balanced Scorecard will prove useful in planning and executing the transition to the Influence

Scorecard, as will the organization's own experiences of its prior transition to the Balanced Scorecard or an equivalent.

Following board approval, I suggest the following actions:

- Form a small steering team – probably formed and overseen by the OSM or equivalent, with representation from marketing, public relations, customer service, operations and HR.
- Approve the draft project plan, or tweak accordingly.
- Develop a role and person specification for the CInflO.
- Recruit the CInflO, transferring to that person responsibility for the transition to the Influence Scorecard – the steering team may continue to act as 'reinforcements'.
- The CInflO finalizes and secures approval for the project plan.
- Execute the project plan.
- The Influence Scorecard and OIPM become operational – an opportunity to pursue the all-important internal communication objectives in this regard.
- The steering team convenes regularly to review progress against plan – perhaps weekly for two quarters, then monthly for two quarters.

As a further plug for the website accompanying this book, it will be great to have Chief Influence Officers and influence professionals drop by regularly to ask questions, provide answers and generally share experiences. I will definitely be hanging out there, of course.

I believe that the Influence Scorecard can only be highly beneficial for an organization and its stakeholders. Rarely is everyone a winner, but I consider that the improvement in your organization's abilities to influence and be influenced must be of great advantage to all – except, perhaps, your competition. I look forward to hearing of your successes.

GLOSSARY OF TERMS

1st / 2nd / 3rd / 4th / 5th / 6th flow – *see* Six Influence Flows.

4 models / the 4th model – describes four views of public relations as defined by James Grunig and Todd Hunt, the 4th being the one advocated by the *Excellence* study: the two-way symmetrical model.

Accessible – easily understood or appreciated; friendly and easy to talk to; approachable.

AMA – American Marketing Association.

AMEC – Association for Measurement and Evaluation of Communication.

APQC – American Productivity and Quality Center.

AVE – Advertising Value Equivalence; a discredited approach to gauging the value of public relations (or media relations more precisely).

Balanced Scorecard – a BPM approach; a management system (not only a measurement system) that enables organizations to clarify their vision and strategy and translate them into action; provides a framework that not only provides performance measurements, but helps planners to identify what should be done and measured.

BPM – Business Performance Management; the disciplined approach to management encompassing metric selection, measurement and organizational learning.

Buyer marketing – individuals market their needs or desires, either directly or anonymously via a streams bank or other broker, to organizations interested in meeting that need or desire; also known as personal RFP (request for proposal).

CCO – Chief Communications Officer, also known as Director of Public Relations or Director of Corporate Communications; more recently, also Chief Customer Officer and Chief Culture Officer.

Chaos – a system exhibiting unpredictability.

CIM – Chartered Institute of Marketing.

CInflO – Chief Influence Officer; runs the OIPM and takes an 'integrator role' in the OSM.

CIO – Chief Information Officer.

CIPR – the UK's Chartered Institute of Public Relations.

Citizen – a legally recognized subject or national of a state or commonwealth with rightful interest or concern in the workings of that nation or state.

Client – a person or organization under the care of another.

CMO – Chief Marketing Officer.

Competitor – an organization with objectives that clash with our own either directly (e.g. fly with us not them) or indirectly (e.g. don't fly, video conference instead).

Complex / complexity – being intricate or complicated (also see Emergence).

COO – Chief Operations Officer.

CPRS – Canadian Public Relations Society.

CRM – Customer Relationship Management; managing an organization's interactions with customers, clients and sales prospects.

C-suite – the term given to the collection of C-titles, such as CEO, COO, CMO, etc.

Customer – a person or organization that buys goods or services (where 'buys' includes paying with one's attention or time; includes 'consumer').

Customer perspective – one of four perspectives of the Balanced Scorecard addressing the question: To achieve our vision, how should we appear to our customers?

CxO – A generic reference to any C-suite title.

Data – discrete, objective facts, signals or symbols devoid of context and interpretation and therefore of no meaning or value.

Digital detritus – the data each and every one of us kicks off as a product or by product of our use of digital products and services.

Emergence / emergent behaviour – a scientific term used to describe how very many relatively simple interactions can give rise to complex systems (i.e. systems that exhibit one or more properties as a whole that aren't manifest for smaller parts or individual components).

Employee – a person employed for wages or salary (taken to include their dependents, and also retired employees still financially reliant upon the organization's ongoing success).

Engage – occupy or attract someone's interest or attention; involve someone in a conversation or discussion (a measurable outcome of influence).

Evaluation – the making of a judgement about the amount, number, or value of something.

Excellence study – the most extensive study of public relations best practice to date.

Financial perspective – one of four perspectives of the Balanced Scorecard addressing the question: To succeed financially, how should we appear to our shareholders?

Focus on the influenced – a component of the influence-centric approach that advocates prioritizing investment of influence resources on those who have already been influenced as you'd intended, rather than those that haven't yet.

For-profit organization – primary motivation is to make and distribute surplus funds to owners.

Human capital – skills, knowledge and values.

ICCO – International Communications Consultancy Association.

IMC – Integrated Marketing Communications; the management of all organized communications to build positive relationships with customers and other stakeholders; stresses marketing to the individual by understanding needs, motivations, attitudes and behaviours.

Influence – you have been influenced when you think in a way you wouldn't otherwise have thought or do something you wouldn't otherwise have done.

Influence-centric – an approach to influence with two foci: one on focusing on the influenced, and the other on tracing influence.

Influence objective – each overarching organizational objective may demand a subset of influence objectives wholly necessary and sufficient in influence terms to accomplish the overarching objective.

Influence performance management – the ease and effectiveness with which we can manage and learn from influence flows; integral to the process by which customers, citizens and all stakeholders interact with organizations and governments to broker mutually valuable, beneficial relationships; a reframing of marketing and PR for the 21st century.

Influence professional – a member of the CInflO's team, of the OIPM.

Influence Scorecard – represents all the differentiated influence processes for incorporation into business performance management (BPM); the subset or view of the Balanced Scorecard (or equivalent) containing all the influence-related KPIs stripped of functional silo; helps to ensure that the full potential to influence and be influenced is exploited cohesively and consistently; the name for our influence framework here, our management approach to setting influence strategy within the purview of the Six Influence Flows and mapping influence strategy.

Influence strategy – describes how an organization expects to influence and be influenced in ways that are wholly necessary and sufficient to the achievement of the influence objectives and successful execution of the overarching strategy; at once part of the overall organizational strategy (for what is an organizational strategy devoid of any aspect of influence?) and driven by it.

Influencer-centric – an approach to influence that pivots around finding and influencing the so-called influencers or 'influentials'; described by the author as an immature approach in comparison to influence-centricity.

Influentials – a name given to select individuals regarded as having the power to influence many others; a focus of Malcolm Gladwell's *The Tipping Point* and the title of a book by Jon Berry and Ed Keller.

Information – the result of structuring or organizing data in such a way as to give it meaning and relevance for specific purpose or in a specific context.

Information capital – systems, databases, networks.

Interaction – reciprocal action or influence.

Internal business processes perspective – one of four perspectives of the Balanced Scorecard addressing the question: To satisfy our shareholders and customers, what business processes must we excel at?

Internet of Things – refers to a network of objects not historically connected: the device containing electronics in order to fulfil its primary function; the electrical device traditionally absent of sophisticated electronics; non-electrical objects; and environmental sensors.

Internetome – the manifestations of the Internet of Things.

Knowledge – the result of structuring or organizing information in such a way that it helps to form a framework for the incorporation of further information and aids the evaluation of the world, accruing experience, expertise and know-how.

KPI – Key Performance Indicator; a performance metric.

Learning and growth perspective – one of four perspectives of the Balanced Scorecard addressing the question: To achieve our vision, how will we sustain our ability to change and improve?

Left-brained – while emerging from scientific study of the brain, we use this term in its non-scientific generalization as meaning 'having a bias towards logic, mathematics and science, detail orientation, systematic thinking'.

Life stream – a term coined by Eric Freeman and David Gelernter at Yale University in the mid-1990s to describe '. . . a time-ordered stream of documents that functions as a diary of your electronic life; every document you create and every document other people send you is stored in your lifestream'.

Linked data – a subtopic of the semantic Web that allows data to be described with reference to universally available common vocabularies.

Marketing – the process by which companies create value for customers and build strong customer relationships in order to capture value from customers in return.

Measurement – the action of measuring something; ascertaining the size, amount, or degree of something by using an instrument or device; assessing the importance, effect, or value of something.

Metric – a system or standard of measurement; (in business) a set of figures or statistics that measure results.

Mission – why an organization exists.

Motivation – reason(s) for acting or behaving in a particular way.

MyChannel – describes a scenario where every single person has her own unique 'channel' made up of her own subscriptions, her friends' subscriptions and recommendations, and automated 'if you like that, you'll like this' discovery.

Net Promoter Score (NPS) – an approach to quantifying customer loyalty and advocacy based on customers' answers to the question: 'Would you feel comfortable recommending us to others?'

Netizens – a portmanteau of Internet and citizen; not 'online publics' in the normal 'digital PR' context, but people who respond to stimuli online.

Non-profit organization – primary motivation is not financial but to achieve some other ends; has a controlling board rather than owners.

OIPM – Office of influence performance management; run by the CInflO, taking responsibility for every aspect of the Six Influence Flows and the Influence Scorecard.

Organization – an organized group of people with a particular purpose.

Organization capital – culture, leadership, alignment, teamwork.

OSM – Office of strategy management; a team specifically charged with executing the strategy processes; specifically in relation to strategy maps and the Balanced Scorecard.

PageRank – According to Google: 'PageRank reflects our view of the importance of web pages by considering more than 500 million variables and 2 billion terms. Pages that we believe are important pages receive a higher PageRank and are more likely to appear at the top of the search results.'

Partner – a person or organization of importance to an organization achieving its objectives (e.g. supplier, reseller, retailer).

Permission marketing – a marketing approach that requires permission to be obtained before advancing to the next step in the purchasing process; coined by Seth Godin; considered to be the opposite of interruption marketing.

Privacy – the ability to determine for ourselves when, how, and to what extent information about us is communicated to others.

Privacy dial – virtual instrumentation allowing easy selection of the privacy option required for a product or service, or group of products or services.

Privacy framework – a simple, universal approach to allowing customers to manage their privacy preferences.

Prospect – a person or organization regarded as a potential customer.

PRSA – Public Relations Society of America.

Public organization – primary motivation set by the state and under the operational control of the state.

Public relations – a management function that focuses on two-way communication and fostering of mutually beneficial relationships between an organization and its publics.

Relationship – the way in which two or more people or things are connected, or the state of being connected.

Relevance – closely connected or appropriate to the matter in hand.

Reputation – the beliefs or opinions that are generally held about someone or something.

Resonance – the power to evoke enduring images, memories, and emotions.

RFID – Radio Frequency Identification; small tags that hold digital information about the item and can be read remotely, and are physically attached to the item in question and can be active (have a battery) but more often these days are passive (no battery).

Right-brained – while emerging from scientific study of the brain, we use this term in its non-scientific generalization as meaning having a bias towards feelings, 'big picture' oriented, images, spatial perception.

ROCI – Return on customer investment; a term invoked by Schultz and Schultz in describing integrated marketing communications.

ROI – Return on investment; a financial calculation determining the likely or actual financial return expected from or delivered by a specific investment.

SBU – Strategic business unit; a unit of the company that has a separate mission and objectives, and that can be planned and evaluated independently from the other parts of the company; an entity with one universal set of influence objectives.

Semantic analysis – computationally trying to determine the meaning of language, of a corpus.

Semantic Web – the Web as a universal medium for data, information and knowledge exchange; where the Web itself understands the meaning of all the content and participation (*see also* Linked Data).

Sentiment analysis – a subtopic of semantic analysis; computationally trying to determine the author's emotional regard for or attitude towards something from the text alone.

SEO – Search engine optimization; the process of editing a webpage to help maximize its PageRank and similar quantifications of its relevance to particular search terms.

Shareholder – an owner of shares in a for-profit organization (taken to include those with other financial holdings or investments contingent upon the organization's financial success).

Significance – the quality of being worthy of attention; importance.

Six Influence Flows – a simple model describing the flows of influence between an organization, its stakeholders and the competition: *1st flow* – our influence with our stakeholders; *2nd flow* – our stakeholders' influence with each other in respect to us; *3rd flow* – our stakeholders' influence with us; *4th flow* – our competitors' influence with our stakeholders; *5th flow* – our stakeholders' influence with each other in respect to our competitors; *6th flow* – our stakeholders' influence with our competition.

Social media – media that isn't traditional / 'industrial' / 'mass' media; facilitates social interaction.

Social Web – consists of social media, applications, services and the network of devices.

Social Web analytics – the application of search, indexing, semantic analysis and business intelligence technologies to the task of identifying, tracking, listening to and participating in the distributed conversations about a particular brand, product or issue, with emphasis on quantifying the trend in each conversation's sentiment and influence.

Stakeholder – a person or organization with an interest or concern in our organization or something our organization is involved in.

Strategy – Michael Porter defines strategy to be about selecting the set of activities in which an organization will excel to create a sustainable difference in the marketplace, and thereby creating sustained value for its shareholders (or sustainable value in the case of non-profits).

Strategy maps – a process developed by Kaplan and Norton; provides the visual framework for integrating the organization's objectives in the four perspectives of a Balanced Scorecard; illustrates the cause-and-effect relationships that link desired outcomes in the customer and financial perspectives to outstanding performance in critical internal processes; and identifies the specific capabilities in the organization's intangible assets that are required for delivering exceptional performance in the critical internal processes.

Streams bank – the service with the primary purpose of collecting all your digital detritus, all your so-called life streams of data, in one place on your behalf and giving you the power to analyse and visualize it all; may offer additional services.

Tracing influence – a component of the influence-centric approach that seeks to understand and learn from how influence has been exerted before; seeks to 'close the loop'.

Trust – firm belief in the reliability, truth, or ability of someone or something.

Values – describes what's important to an organization.

Vision – describes what an organization wants to be.

VRM – Vendor relationship management; a project exploring how customers may be given the same capabilities in managing their relationships with vendors as vendors have today for managing their customer relations (with customer relationship management, CRM, systems).

Web 1.0 – sometimes referred to as the transactional Web; dominated by read-only websites and ecommerce.

Web 2.0 – the advent of the Web characterized by (user generated) content and community (social) participation (*see also* Social media).

Web 3.0 – commonly taken to mean the semantic Web (*see also* Semantic Web).

Web of data – *see also* Semantic Web.

Wisdom – my favourite definition of wisdom is the ability to make information super-useful; described as an amalgam of knowledge and judgement, resulting in 'know-why' in the form of 'why do' (rather than in the form of 'why is', which is information).

ENDNOTES

1 Search Engine Strategies 2009 Conference, Chicago: http://ebusiness-unibw. org/pipermail/goodrelations/2009-December/000152.html

2 RFID describes a technology whereby small unpowered tags are attached to non-electrical things, and remote reading devices can then power and communicate with the tags from a distance, usually with the intention of learning about the thing and tracking its movements. For more information see http://en. wikipedia.org/wiki/rfid

3 http://www.cluetrain.com/book/index.html

4 *Permission Marketing*, Seth Godin, Simon & Schuster, 1999, ISBN: 9780684856360

5 Conversion factor of 1.284 from http://oregonstate.edu/cla/polisci/sites/default/ files/faculty-research/sahr/inflation-conversion/pdf/cv1999.pdf

6 http://www.tns-mi.com/news/03202001.htm

7 http://www.kantarmediana.com/news/03172010.htm

8 http://techcrunch.com/2009/03/22/why-advertising-is-failing-on-the-internet

9 Hugh MacLeod, http://gapingvoid.com, reproduced with permission

10 http://online.wsj.com/article/SB116925820512582318.html Bret Swanson, 'The Coming Exaflood,' *Wall Street Journal*, 20 January 2007

11 http://www.youtube.com/user/TheRoyalChannel

12 http://www.nytimes.com/2006/10/09/business/media/09adcol.html

13 *The New Rules of Marketing and PR*, David Meerman Scott, Wiley, 2007, 9780470113455

14 Marketing and the 7Ps, The Chartered Institute of Marketing, 2009

15 Agenda Paper – *Tomorrow's World: re-evaluating the role of marketing*, The Chartered Institute of Marketing, 2007

16 *Principles of Marketing* (5th European edn), Philip Kotler, Gary Armstrong, Veronica Wong, John Saunders, 2008, Pearson Education, ISBN: 9780273711568

17 http://twoscenarios.typepad.com/maneuver_marketing_commun/2008/01/ everything-that.html

18   Ibid. 14

19   Ibid. 15

20   http://toughsledding.wordpress.com/2008/07/24/what-public-relations-is-not

21   http://www.prconversations.com/index.php/2007/06/anne-gregory-on-relationships-between-public-relations-and-journalism

22   *Managing Public Relations*, James Grunig and Todd Hunt, 1984, Wadsworth Publishing, ISBN: 9780030583377

23   *Excellent public relations and effective organizations: A Study of Communication Management in Three Countries*, Routledge, ISBN: 9780805818185, reproduced with permission

24   PRSA   1982   National   Assembly   http://www.prsa.org/AboutPRSA/PublicRelationsDefined

25   http://definingpublicrelations.wikispaces.com

26   'Introducing a new, maple-infused definition of public relations, in both official languages', Judy Gombita, PR Conversations, 17th June 2009, http://www.prconversations.com/index.php/2009/06/introducing-a-new-maple-infused-definition-of-public-relations

27   Ibid. 23

28   The Engineering of Consent, 1947, *The Annals of the American Academy of Political and Social Science*, 250, p. 113

29   *Information, Influence & Communication: A Reader in Public Relations*, Otto Lerbinger, Albert J. Sullivan, 1965

30   *Paradigms of global public relations in an age of digitalisation*, James Grunig, 2009, http://praxis.massey.ac.nz/fileadmin/Praxis/Files/globalPR/GRUNIG.pdf, PRism 6(2)

31   Ibid. 23

32   *Integrated Marketing Communications: Putting It Together and Making It Work*, Don E. Schultz, Stanley I. Tannenbaum, Robert F. Lauterborn, McGraw-Hill, 1993, ISBN: 9780844233635, reproduced with permission

33   http://www.medill.northwestern.edu/imc

34   *IMC – The Next Generation: Five steps for delivering value and measuring returns using marketing communications*, Don E. Schultz and Heidi F. Schultz, 2003, McGraw-Hill, ISBN: 0071416625

35   *Integrated Marketing Communications: Best Practices Report*, American Productivity and Quality Center, Houston: APQC, 1998

36   *Communicating Globally: An Integrated Marketing Approach*, Don E. Schultz and Philip J. Kitchen, 2000, NTC Business Books

37   Question: In brief, what is your definition of and regard for 'integrated marketing'? Responses submitted September and October 2010

38   Ibid. 30

39 *Putting the Public Back in Public Relations: How social media is reinventing the aging business of PR*, Brian Solis and Deirdre Breakenridge, 2009, Upper Saddle River, NJ: Pearson Education

40 *Online Public Relations: A practical guide to developing an online strategy in the world of social media*, David Phillips and Philip Young, 2009, Kogan Page

41 Ibid. 40

42 http://en.wikipedia.org/wiki/Complex_system

43 http://www.theregister.co.uk/2001/06/30/michael_hauben_netizen_dies

44 http://www.briansolis.com/2010/08/please-repeat-influence-is-not-popularity

45 http://www.philipsheldrake.com/2010/03/influence-the-bullshit-best-practice-and-promise

46 *Influencer Grudge Match: Lady Gaga versus Bono – What makes an influencer?*, Brian Solis and Frank Strong, September 2010, http://www.vocus.com/social-media/influencer/what-makes-an-influencer.pdf

47 http://www.briansolis.com/2010/08/social-media%E2%80%99s-critical-path-relevance-to-resonance-to-significance

48 http://econsultancy.com/uk/blog/4887-35-social-media-kpis-to-help-measure-engagement

49 *Are we engaged yet? How to develop your engagement metric*, Katie Delahaye Paine, presentation to Monitoring Social Media 2010, 6 October 2010. http://www.kdpaine.com/index.cfm/all-about-katie-delahaye-paine/katies-speech-archives

50 Disclosure: the author has a commercial interest in Taptu

51 The Marketing Century: How Marketing Drives Business and Shapes Society, Chartered Institute of Marketing, 2011, Wiley, ISBN: 9780470660157

52 http://www.philipsheldrake.com/2009/04/there-is-no-such-thing-as-a-twitter-strategy-but-you-should-have-clear-expectations-for-your-corporate-twitter-profile

53 http://www.socialwebanalytics.com

54 http://www.socialtarget.com

55 http://www.altimetergroup.com/2010/04/altimeter-report-social-marketing-analytics-with-web-analytics-demystified.html

56 *Real-Time Marketing & PR: How to instantly engage your market, connect with customers, and create products that grow your business now*, David Meerman Scott, 2010, Wiley, ISBN: 9780470645956

57 http://www.webanalyticsassociation.org

58 http://www.smartinsights.com/wp-content/uploads/2009/12/Listening-Platforms-Update-20.01.10-PDF-version.pdf

59 Or more precisely, what database engineers refer to as extraction, transformation and loading (ETL)

60 http://www.holmesreport.com/blog/index.cfm/2010/6/21/A-Stake-Through-the-Heart-of-Advertising-Value-Equivalency

61 *Measure What Matters: Online Tools For Understanding Customers, Social Media, Engagement, and Key Relationships*, Katie Delahaye Paine, Wiley, 2011, ISBN: 9780470920107

62 http://klout.com/kscore

63 http://en.wikipedia.org/wiki/Network_science

64 Committee on Network Science for Future Army Applications, National Research Council, Network Science, ISBN: 9780309100267, p. 28, http://www.nap.edu/openbook.php?record_id=11516&page=28

65 http://www.ipa.co.uk/Content/Results-of-third-IPA-TouchPoints-Survey

66 Making Social Networks Profitable, *Business Week*, 25 August 2008 http://www.businessweek.com/magazine/content/08_40/b4102050681705.htm

67 http://www.searchenginepeople.com/blog/influencerank-googles-social-media-PageRank.html

68 http://www.PostRank.com

69 http://www.speedcommunications.com/blogs/wadds/2010/08/10/ellie-and-freya-on-agency-life-pr-and-their-influences

70 http://youtube/onaapqbCXQ8 8 minutes 10 seconds in

71 *Fluent: The Razorfish Social Influence Marketing Report*, Razorfish, 2009, http://fluent.razorfish.com, reproduced with permission

72 *Consumers Pushing Companies into Social Media*, Invoke Solutions, August 2010, http://www.invoke.com/index/08-04-10

73 *Speak Now or Forever Hold Your Tweets*, Harris Interactive, 3rd June 2010, Table 5 http://www.harrisinteractive.com/vault/HI-Harris-Poll-Opinions-In-Social-Media-2010-06-03.pdf

74 *The Tipping Point: How Little Things Can Make a Big Difference*, Malcolm Gladwell, Little Brown, 2000, ISBN: 0316316962

75 *Social Circles*, Paul Adams, New Riders, ISBN: 9780321719645

76 http://www.slideshare.net/padday/bridging-the-gap-between-our-online-and-offline-social-network slides 131–140

77 Determining Influential Users in Internet Social Networks, August 2010, *Journal of Marketing Research*, Dr Michael Trusov, Assistant Professor of Marketing at the Robert H. Smith School of Business at the University of Maryland, Dr Anand Bodapati, Associate Professor in the Anderson School of Management at the University of California, and Dr Randolf E. Bucklin, Professor of Marketing in the Anderson School of Management at the University of California. http://bit.ly/influentialusers

78 http://www.fastcompany.com/magazine/122/is-the-tipping-point-toast.html?page=0%2C1, reproduced with permission

79 *The Influentials: One American in Ten Tells the Other Nine How to Vote, Where to Eat, and What to Buy*, Jon Berry and Ed Keller, Free Press, 2003, ISBN: 9780743227292

80 http://mashable.com/2010/08/10/personalized-news-stream
81 I recognize that chaotic systems are mathematically deterministic too, but this isn't a mathematical text and expanding on such detail wouldn't have added anything to the assertion but may have diluted the message or lost the reader's attention
82 *The Ultimate Question*, Fred Reichheld, Cambridge, MA: Harvard Business School Press, 2001, ISBN: 9781591397830
83 Jim Novo's review of *Firm-Created Word-of-Mouth Communication: Evidence from a Field Test*, Godes, David, Mayzlin, Dina, 2009, i, Vol. 28, No. 4.: http://www.webanalyticsassociation.org/members/blog_view.asp?id=538344&post=89776
84 *Strategy Maps: Converting Intangible Assets into Tangible Outcomes*, Robert S. Kaplan and David P. Norton, 2004, Harvard Business School Publishing Corporation, ISBN: 9781591391340
85 http://dvd-rent-test.dreamhost.com/#why
86 http://blog.netflix.com/2010/03/friends-update.html
87 An interview with Katie Delahaye Paine, Philip Sheldrake, May 2010, http://www.cipr.co.uk/content/cipr-social-media-measurement-group-launches
88 *Wisdom of Crowds: Why the Many Are Smarter Than the Few and How Collective Wisdom Shapes Business, Economies, Societies and Nations*, James Surowiecki, Doubleday, 2004, ISBN: 9780385503860
89 http://www.inc.com/magazine/20060901/hidi-hsieh.html
90 http://www.balancedscorecard.org/BSCResources/AbouttheBalancedScorecard/tabid/55/Default.aspx
91 *Balanced Scorecard: Translating Strategy into Action*, Robert S. Kaplan and David P. Norton, 1996, Harvard Business School Publishing Corporation, ISBN: 9780875846514
92 *Strategy Maps: Converting Intangible Assets into Tangible Outcomes*, Robert S. Kaplan and David P. Norton, 2004, Harvard Business School Publishing Corporation, ISBN: 9781591391340, reproduced with permission
93 *The Execution Premium: Linking Strategy to Operations for Competitive Advantage*, Robert S. Kaplan and David P. Norton, 2008, Harvard Business School Publishing Corporation, ISBN: 9781422121160
94 The Office of Strategy Management, Robert S. Kaplan and David P. Norton, *Harvard Business Review*, October 2005, pp. 72–80, reproduced with permission
95 http://blogs.hbr.org/hbr/kaplan-norton/2008/08/strategy-execution-needs-a-sys.html
96 *The Essential Bennis*, Warren Bennis with Patricia Ward Biederman, Wiley, 2009, p. 210, ISBN: 9780470432396
97 http://www.balancedscorecard.org/BSCResources/AbouttheBalancedScorecard/Definitions/tabid/145/Default.aspx

98 *Socialize the Enterprise*, John Bell, Ogilvy & Mather, July 2010, http://www. slideshare.net/OgilvyWW/socialize-the-enterprise, reproduced with permission

99 Inventing the 21st-century purchasing organization, Chip Hardt, Nicolas Reinecke, and Peter Spiller, *McKinsey Quarterly*, November 2007, http://www. mckinseyquarterly.com/Inventing_the_21st-century_purchasing_organization_ 2053

100 http://twitter.com/#!/Sheldrake/statuses/26647395898

101 *Social Media Metrics: how to measure and optimize your marketing measurement*, Jim Sterne, 2010, Wiley, ISBN: 9780470583784

102 *Measure What Matters: Online Tools For Understanding Customers, Social Media, Engagement, and Key Relationships*, Katie Delahaye Paine, Wiley,February 2011, ISBN: 9780470920107

103 *Marketing Metrics: The Definitive Guide to Measuring Marketing Performance*, Paul W. Farris, Neil T. Bendle, Phillip E. Pfeifer, David J. Reibstein, 2010, Wharton School Publishing, ISBN: 9780137058297

104 *Balanced Scorecard: Translating Strategy into Action*, Robert S. Kaplan and David P. Norton, 1996, Harvard Business School Publishing Corporation, ISBN: 9780875846514

105 http://kpilibrary.com

106 http://www.smartkpis.com

107 http://www.kpi-portal.com

108 http://www.bsccommunity.com

109 http://www.thepalladiumgroup.com/communities/XPC

110 By-invitation conference call with AMEC, PRSA, CIPR, PRCA, 25 October 2010

111 http://www.amecorg.com

112 David Meerman Scott being interviewed about ROI by Ricardo Bueno and Stacey Soleil, January 2010, http://www.webinknow.com/2010/01/roi-rant.html

113 Twitter, Twitter, Little Stars, *Business Week*, 19 July–25 July 2010, by Felix Gillette

114 http://marketingmeasurementtoday.blogspot.com

115 http://marketingmeasurementtoday.blogspot.com/2010/09/measurement-problems-check-your.html

116 http://marketingmeasurementtoday.blogspot.com/2009/07/twittering-away-time-and-money.html

117 *Chaotics: The Business of Managing and Marketing in the Age of Turbulence*, Philip Kotler and John A. Caslione, 2009, American Management Association, ISBN: 9780814415214

118 *IMC – The Next Generation: Five steps for delivering value and measuring returns using marketing communications*, Don E. Schultz and Heidi F. Schultz, 2003, McGraw-Hill, ISBN: 0071416625, reproduced with permission

119 *The Future for Marketing Capability*, The Chartered Institute of Marketing and Accenture, http://www.cim.co.uk/shop/books/bookDetails/Futuremarketing. aspx, September 2010

120 Ibid. 118

121 *Business @ the Speed of Thought*, Bill Gates, Penguin, 2000, ISBN: 9780140283129

122 Who Owns You? Piers Bizony, *Engineering & Technology*, Vol. 5 Issue 11, The Institution of Engineering and Technology, July 2010

123 Mozilla, the organization behind the popular Firefox browser, recognizes this issue as a bug and provided a fix in 2010 for subsequent incorporation into a new version of the browser. If and when this update is rolled out in Firefox, and if and when other browsers are updated equally, this website may no longer work as intended, and indeed may be withdrawn altogether

124 http://blogs.law.harvard.edu/doc/2010/07/31/the-data-bubble

125 http://blogs.wsj.com/wtk

126 *Authenticity: What Consumers Really Want*, James Gilmore and Joseph Pine, Harvard Business School Press, 2007, ISBN: 9781591391456

127 http://plato.stanford.edu/entries/privacy

128 http://en.wikipedia.org/wiki/Attention_economy

129 http://projectvrm.org

130 http://themineproject.org

131 http://www.kantarainitiative.org

132 http://cyber.law.harvard.edu/projectvrm/Personal_RFP

133 http://www.dilbert.com/blog/entry/hunter_becomes_the_prey

134 http://richard.cyganiak.de/2007/10/lod/lod-datasets_2010-09-22.html

135 http://www.philipsheldrake.com/2010/08/intro-to-web-3-0-and-the-internet-of-things-at-the-cipr-social-summer-session

136 http://ebusiness-unibw.org/pipermail/goodrelations/2009-December/000152. html

137 http://googlewebmastercentral.blogspot.com/2009/05/introducing-rich-snip-pets.html

138 http://techcrunch.com/2010/04/21/no-jcpr-edelman-im-not-taking-that-iphone-survey-story-down

139 http://www.marketingmagazine.co.uk/news/1014546/M-C-Saatchi-rejigs-PR-arm-launches-consumer-corporate-division

140 http://www.prweek.com/uk/news/1016107/Comms-Directors-Survey-Weve-turned-corner

141 http://www.prweek.com/uk/news/search/903849/Media-agencies-muscle

142 http://en.wikipedia.org/wiki/United_Breaks_Guitars

143 http://www.businessweek.com/magazine/content/10_39/b4196007421255. htm

144 Rethinking Marketing, Roland Trust, Christine Moorman, Gaurav Bhalla, *Harvard Business Review*, January 2010

145 An interview with Brian Solis, Philip Sheldrake, July 2010, http://www.philip-sheldrake.com/2010/07/an-interview-with-brian-solis

146 An interview with Katie Delahaye Paine, Philip Sheldrake, May 2010, http://www.cipr.co.uk/content/cipr-social-media-measurement-group-launches

147 *The Authentic Enterprise*, Arthur W. Page Society, 2007, http://www.awpagesociety.com/site/resources/white_papers

148 *Marketing Metrics: The Definitive Guide to Measuring Marketing Performance*, Paul W. Farris, Neil T. Bendle, Phillip E. Pfeifer, David J. Reibstein, 2010, Wharton School Publishing, ISBN: 9780137058297, reproduced with permission

149 Agenda Paper – *Tomorrow's World: Re-evaluating the role of marketing*, The Chartered Institute of Marketing, 2007

150 *The CMO-CIO Alignment Imperative: Driving revenue through customer relevance*, CMO Council, Business Performance Innovation Network, Accenture, October 2010

151 Rethinking Marketing, Roland Trust, Christine Moorman, Gaurav Bhalla, *Harvard Business Review*, January 2010

152 *Chief Culture Officer: How to create a living, breathing corporation*, Grant McCracken, Basic Books, January 2010, ISBN: 9780465018321

153 http://en.wikipedia.org/wiki/Corporate_title

INDEX

Index compiled by Sophia Clapham

408268